SE

MENU

RECIPES

CHINESE RESTAURANT MENU RECIPES

S ALLIE M ORRIS

foulsham
LONDON • NEW YORK • TORONTO • SYDNEY

foulsham

The Publishing House
Bennetts Close,
Cippenham, Berks SL1 5AP

ISBN 0-572-01776-6

Typeset in Great Britain by Typesetting Solutions, Slough, Berks.
Printed in Great Britain by St. Edmundsbury Press, Bury St. Edmunds, Suffolk.

CHINESE
RESTAURANT
MENU

FOO LO SHAM

Appetisers

Prawn and Crispy Noodle Balls . . 41

X I A   M E I N   W A N   Z I

*Luxurious parcels of ocean fresh prawn and fish wrapped
with a coating of delicious deep-fried crushed noodles*

❧

Crispy Shanghai Spring Rolls. . . 42

C U I   P I   S H A N G H A I   C H U N   J U A N

*Hot crispy pancakes with a juicy stuffing of pork, prawns,
Chinese mushroom, or vegetarian beancurd, and packed
with crunchy bamboo shoots, bean sprouts and exotic water
chestnuts*

❧

Vegetarian Spring Rolls 43

S H U   C H U N   J U A N

*A hint of ginger adds spice to this tasty concoction of onions,
carrots, bean sprouts, water chestnuts and bamboo shoots*

❧

Fried Crispy Wontons with
Apricot Dipping Sauce 44

G U O   Z H I   Z H A   W O N   T O N

*Crisp mouthfuls stuffed with pork, prawns and spring
onions and served with a zingy sweet and sour apricot dip*

❧

Salt and Pepper Prawns 46

J I A O   Y A N   X I A

*Succulent king prawns marinated in your own special
sweet and spicy sauce of garlic, chilli and shallots – with a
touch of ginger*

Crispy Fried Seaweed 47

CAI SUNG

*China's most delectable deception – not seaweed at all, but
finely shredded deep-fried spring greens, dusted with sugar
and sesame seeds*

Steamed Mussels with
Black Bean Sauce 48

SI ZHI QING TAI BEI

*The light scent of the sea blended with the saltiness of your
oyster and black bean sauce, with a contrasting garnish of
spring onion*

Sunshine and Snowflake Toasts . . 50

CHI MA XIA TU SSU

*Tiny golden crispy toasts lightly sprinkled with snow-white
sesame seeds*

Barbecued Pork Spareribs 51

MI ZHI SHAO PAI GU

Smoky, spicy and finger-licking tasty

Lettuce Parcels 52

SHENG CAI BAO

*Intriguing packets of pleasure touched with savoury hoisin
sauce tumble open to reveal a spicy pork filling blended
with crisp bamboo shoots, crunchy water chestnuts and
peanuts*

Scrambled Eggs with Mushrooms in Pancakes 54

MU HSU R'OU

Velvety scrambled egg, textured with mushrooms, bamboo shoots, ginger and shreds of pork, packs these delicious Mandarin pancakes

❀

Cantonese Egg Foo Yung 56

SHI JIN FU RON

A rustic omelette, filled with roast pork, bean sprouts, water chestnuts and delicate shredded Chinese leaves

❀

Tea Eggs 57

CH'A YEH TAN

After a thousand years, discover the simple secret of these beautifully marbled eggs

Dim Sum

Steamed Flower Rolls 60

HUA JUAN

Hot soft steamed rolls, traditionally served with Aromatic Crispy Duck

❀

Steamed Pork Buns 61

ROU BAOZI

Moist and fluffy steamed buns with a pork filling, spiced with a yellow bean sauce

Turnip Paste Squares 62

LAW PAK GO

*Delicious packages of moolie paste, subtly flavoured with
Chinese sausage and dried prawns, then quickly fried till
crisp and golden brown*

※

Steamed Buns with
Pork and Prawn Stuffing 63

SUI MAI

*Moist and fluffy steamed buns with a pork, prawn and
ginger filling*

※

Soy and Vinegar Dip 64

JIANG CU YU

A rich, tangy dip

※

Soy and Garlic Dip 64

SUAN JIANG YU

*Less tangy than the Soy and Vinegar Dip, but equally
delicious*

Soups

Pork Ball and Watercress Soup . . 66

ROU WAN YANG CAI TANG

*Peppery fresh watercress emphasises the subtle flavour of
pork balls, with cellophane noodles*

Peking Duck Soup with Three Vegetables 67

YA ROU SAN SI TANG

Celery, leek and shredded Chinese leaves enhance a delicious clear duck soup

❧

Hot and Sour Soup 68

SUAN LA TANG

A kaleidoscope of oriental flavours in a typically spicy Chinese soup

❧

Wonton Soup 70

WONTON TANG

Tiny, delicately flavoured pork and ginger dumplings floating in a clear soup garnished with fresh young spinach leaves

❧

Chicken and Sweetcorn Soup . . . 71

JI TI YUMI TANG

A creamy combination of golden corn and morsels of chicken with spring onion

❧

Beancurd Soup with Variations . . 72

SHI JIN DAO FU TANG

Clear home-made stock as a base for a limitless range of soup sensations

❧

Egg Drop Soup with Spinach . . . 73

PO CAI DAN FUA TANG

Another all-time favourite, a good stock is lightly thickened and then beaten egg drizzled in at the last moment to form attractive and delicious 'threads'

Seafood

Stir-Fry Scallops with Mangetout and Garlic 75

XUE DAO CHAO DAIZI

Plump tender scallops coated in a velvety soy and rice wine sauce

Braised Carp 76

HONG SHAO LI YU

The classic Chinese fresh water fish braised whole in the traditional style, with ginger, garlic, onion, soy, chilli, coriander and rice wine

Fried Fish with Green and White Vegetables . . . 78

WU LIU YU

Lightly fried marinated strips of fresh fish tossed together with separately cooked country vegetables at the last minute for a delicious contrast in tastes and textures

Fish Strips with Corn and Straw Mushrooms 80

CAO GU YUMI YU TIA

Bite-sized morsels of fish tenderly simmered in a rich ginger broth and garnished with straw mushrooms, spring onions and sweetcorn, drizzled with sesame oil

Steamed Sea Bass or Sea Trout . . 82

QING ZHENG YU

Mouthwatering tastes and textures enhanced through this delicate process

❀

Red Snapper with Sweet and Sour Sauce 83

TANG CU CHOU YU

Rich flavours blend and contrast to produce seafood with a bite!

❀

Szechuan Prawns 85

GAN SHAO MING XIA

Tiger prawns stir-fried in an authentic Szechuan peppercorn, ginger and rice wine vinegar sauce

❀

Phoenix Tail Prawns 86

FENG WEI XIA

Jumbo prawns marinated in a special sauce, dipped in a featherlight batter and deep-fried

❀

Squid and Black Bean Sauce . . . 88

SI JIAO YOU YU

A rich combination of black beans, garlic, chilli, ginger and soy sauce with succulent squid

❀

Ketchup Fish 90

QUIZI SHAO YU

Not ketchup as you know it – ketchup is the original Chinese word for the delicious blend of soy and oyster sauces which coat this delicately steamed whole fish

Kung Pao Prawn 92

KUNG PO XIA

Crispy fried prawns with spicy Szechuan sauce

❀

Steamed Scallops with
Black Bean Sauce 94

SI ZI ZHENG ZIAN BI

*Scandalously scrumptious steamed scallops in a subtle
sauce, seasoned with sugar, soy, sesame oil and Chinese
wine, elegantly garnished with garlic, spring onion and
coriander leaves*

❀

Duck

Stir-fry Roast Duck
with Bean Sprouts 97

DAO YA CHAO YA

*Morsels of roast duckling quickly stir-fried with onion and
crispy bean sprouts, sprinkled with rice wine
and oyster sauce*

❀

Emperor's Peking Duck 98

BEIJING KAO JA

*Opulent, fragrant, crisp and rich without oiliness – since
time immemorial, a dish fit for an emperor. Crisp skin and
meat wrapped in Mandarin pancakes moistened with
hoisin sauce, filled with a julienne of cucumber and spring
onions*

Aromatic Crispy Duck 100

XIANG SU YA

*Tender young duckling, marinated then deep-fried at the
last minute for a truly crispy skin*

❀

Tea-smoked Roast Duckling . . . 102

ZHAGCHA YAZI

*A rare and unusual flavour to partner the rich delicacy of
crispy roast duckling*

❀

Kaifeng Soy Duck 104

JIANG YA

*Lean and tender pieces of braised duckling served in a rich
deep golden brown sauce*

❀

Steamed Duck Breasts with Pineapple and Preserved Ginger . . 106

ZILO YA SI

*Succulent duck breasts smothered in a fruity sauce studded
with colourful pieces of red peppers, ginger, green peppers
and pineapple*

❀

Sautéed Fillet of Duck with Black Bean Sauce 108

SI ZHI YA PIAN

*Marinated strips of duckling breast flash fried and
smothered in a rich glaze of mixed vegetables
and black beans*

Stir-fry Roast Duck with Lychees. . 110

LYCHEE CHAO YA

An unusual contrast of textures and flavours: strips of roast duckling fried with ginger, mangetout and lychees

Roast Honey Duck 111

SHAO YA

An ambrosial marinade of rice wine, soy sauce, sugar and honey blended to accentuate the rich dark flavour of roast duck

Mandarin Pancakes. 112

BAO BING

Transparently delicious wheaten pancakes

Chicken

Paper-wrapped Chicken 114

ZHI BAO JI

Marinated strips of chicken deep-fried in paper parcels with ham and spring onion

Bang Bang Chicken 116

BON BON JI

Thin slices of poached chicken presented on a bed of cucumber with a tangy peanut sauce, drizzled with chilli oil

Szechuan-style Chicken with Tangerine Peel and Spices 118

CHEN PI JI

Chicken on the bone first marinated, then deep fried, then cooked in a rich, spicy sauce

Sweet and Sour Chicken 120

TANG CU JI

Succulent chicken breasts stir-fried and served in a fruit sauce studded with colourful pieces of red peppers, carrot, green peppers, water chestnuts and pineapple

Chicken with Cashew Nuts . . . 122

YAOGUA CHAO JIN DING

Slender golden slices of choice chicken combined with spring onions, mangetout and button mushrooms in a light soy flavoured sauce with shallow fried cashew nuts, garnished with crispy chicken skin, cashews and coriander

Diced Chicken with Peppers and Yellow Bean Sauce 123

CHING CHIAO JI DING

Tender morsels of chicken stir-fried and served in a spicy bean, pepper and mushroom sauce

Ginger Chicken 125

CONG YOU JI

Plump chicken infused with the lusciously complex flavour of ginger and served with a luxurious brandy, mushroom and coriander sauce

Cantonese Lemon Chicken . . . 126

NING MENG JI

*Piquant citrus sauce adds a tang to the rich moist flavour
of steamed chicken garnished with coriander
and green pepper*

Cantonese Stir-fry Chicken with Mushrooms and Bamboo Shoots . . 128

SHUANG DONG JI QIU

*Slivers of chicken breast stir-fried in a light sauce with straw
mushrooms, Chinese leaves and bamboo shoots, finally
drizzled with hot sesame oil before serving*

Chicken Cubes with Kung Po Sauce . 130

KIUNG PO JI DING

*Juicy chunks of tender chicken marinated in a rich chilli
flavoured sauce and served with golden peanuts*

Lettuce Wrap from the Panda Restaurant 132

SANG CHOY

*Minced chicken with Chinese mushroom and water
chestnuts tossed with deep-fried noodles, then spooned into
parcels of crispy lettuce leaves with a touch of hoisin sauce*

Chilli Chicken 134

LAZI JI

A powerful and pleasantly perfumed preparation of poultry

Spiced Chicken Drumsticks . . 136

WU XIAN JI TUI

*Meaty drumsticks rubbed with aromatic five-spice powder,
simmered till tender in a hot wine and soy sauce and
served with crunchy cool cucumber*

❀

Beef and Lamb

Stir-fry Beef with Oyster Sauce . . 138

HAO YOU NIU ROU

*Paper thin slices cooked in a flash with ginger and green
onions, and served with oyster sauce*

❀

Spiced Shredded Fried Beef . . . 140

GAN CHAO NIU SI

*Matchsticks of beef marinated and stir-fried with 'carrot
flowers' and garnished with fresh chilli*

❀

Ginger Beef with Snow Peas . . . 141

SHI CAI CHAI NIU PIAN

*Richly flavoured mangetout contrasts with the piquancy of
this tender spiced beef*

❀

Beef with Green Peppers
and Black Bean Sauce 142

SI JIAO NIU ROU

*Tasty strips of prime beef coated with a special full
flavoured black bean sauce contrasting with crunchy green
peppers*

Lamb in Lettuce Parcels from the Kaifeng 143

YANG ROU SHENG CAI BAO

Succulent marinated shoulder of lamb steamed, deep-fried to crisp up the skin then served wrapped in crispy lettuce parcels

Stir-fried Lamb with Leeks . . . 145

CONG BAO YANG ROU

Slices of tender young lamb marinated in a potent preparation of five-spice powder, soy, sesame and gin, stir-fried with finely sliced leeks

Pork

Roast Pork Fillet 147

MI ZI CHAR SUI

Delicious hot or cold, a tender fillet of pork marinated in rice wine, honey, hoisin and soy sauces and roasted to a rich mahogany hue

Braised Lion Heads 148

SHI ZI TOU

A typical Shanghai delicacy, made from real lions (only kidding) – made from shredded pork shaped into balls like lion's heads, then braised with vitamin-rich cabbage and served with spinach and noodles

Twice Cooked Pork 150

HUI GUO ROU

*Gently poached slices of tender pork refried with a spicy
Szechuan sauce with bamboo shoots, spring onions and
sesame oil*

❀

Sweet and Sour Pork 152

GU LUO ROU

*The classic Chinese dish, a mouthwatering combination of
exotic flavours that make it everybody's favourite*

❀

Pork and Cloud Ear Pancakes . . 154

MU·SHU·RON

*A heavenly mixture of juicy minced pork and fluffy
scrambled egg with the exotic addition of wild cloud ear
mushrooms, ginger and bamboo shoots, rolled up in
Mandarin pancakes and served with a yellow bean dip*

❀

Red-cooked Aubergine
with Roast Pork 156

YU HSIANG GAIZI

*Deep-fried cubes of aubergine simmered in a Szechuan
sauce of Chinese mushrooms, bamboo shoots and
matchsticks of roast pork, garnished with chilli*

❀

Shredded Pork with
Szechuan Pickled Vegetable . . . 157

ZHA CAI ROU SI

*Marinated pork stir-fried with tangy shreds of pickled
cabbage, tossed with sesame oil and sprinkled with sesame
seeds*

Vegetables

Vegetarian Four Treasures . . . 159

CHAO SU SI BAO

*Chinese mushrooms, mangetout, baby sweetcorn and water
chestnuts quickly stir-fried and served with
a light glazed sauce*

Buddhist Monk's
Vegetable Creation 160

LO HAN ZHAI MATAR PANEER

*A serene mix of crisp and crunchy garden fresh vegetables
with the addition of chunks of fried bean curd*

Ma Po's Beancurd in Hot Sauce . . 162

MA PO DAO FU

*A choice of ingredients – pork or fish – mingled with spicy
hot sauce, beancurd, pickled cabbage and mangetout,
sprinkled with sesame oil and garnished with spring onions*

Stir-fried Mustard Greens
with Oyster Sauce 164

HAO YOU GAILAN

*Mustard greens stir-fried in a moment and flavoured with
tasty oyster sauce and Chinese mushrooms*

Spicy Sweet and Sour Cabbage . . 165

TANG CU PAN BAICAI

*The most exciting way ever to serve healthy, nutritious
Chinese leaves, with the addition of Szechuan peppercorns
and shreds of fresh ginger and chilli*

❧

Snow Peas and Straw Mushrooms . 166

XUE DAO HUI CAO GU

*Served in a smooth melding of oyster, soy sauce and rice
wine*

❧

French Beans with
Bamboo Shoots and Chicken Oil . 167

JI YOU DONGSUN

A sensual combination of textures drizzled with chicken oil

❧

Cantonese Stir-fry Vegetables . . 168

SU SHI JIN

*Oriental colours and textures combine for a real
gourmet's delight*

❧

Stir-fry Mixed Vegetables 169

CHAO SHI CAI

*Spinach, mangetout, 'carrot flowers', water chestnuts and
prawns, garnished with spring onions or coriander*

❧

Spicy Szechuan-style Aubergine . 170

YU XIANG QIEZI

*Chunks of fried aubergine simmered in a rich spicy sauce
and served hot or cold*

Hot and Sour Cucumbers 171

S U N A   L A   C H I N   G U A

*Delicately cooked dwarf cucumbers with chilli and ginger
served with a softly thickened sweet and sour sauce and
sprinkled with sesame seeds*

Rice and Noodles

Egg Fried Rice 174

D A N   C H A O   F A N

*Stir-fried rice speckled with scrambled egg and decorated
with spring onion*

Special Fried Rice 175

S H I   J I N   C H A O   F A N

*A luxurious egg fried rice, with the added ingredients of
prawns, slices of Chinese sausage, Chinese mushrooms,
slivers of roast pork, peas, chilli and spring onion served
with a crisp green fringe of shredded lettuce*

Shredded Chicken Fried Rice with Crispy Lettuce 177

J I   S I   C H A O   F A N

*Another sophisticated egg fried rice with the addition of strips
of chicken and shredded lettuce speedily mingled and fried*

Mandarin Noodles 178

LIANG BAN MEIN

*Cool noodles with cucumber, bean sprouts and spring
onion tossed with a soy dressing and garnished with spring
onions and sesame seeds*

Szechuan Noodles with Peanut Sauce and Vegetables 179

DANG DANG MEIN

*Soft noodles tossed in a peanut and sesame sauce and
presented with a choice of vegetables*

Egg Noodles with Roast Pork . . 181

CHAR SUI TANG MEIN

*Soft egg noodles with your choice of strips of roast pork or
duck, with bean sprouts, shredded stir-fried cabbage and
Chinese sauces, served with a garnish of chilli
and spring onion*

Fried Noodles with Shredded Roast Duck 182

SHAO YA CHOW MEIN

*Stir-fried shreds of roast duck with leeks, celery and ginger
tossed with fried noodles and garnished with a selection
of vegetables*

Desserts

Peking Dust 185

LI TZE FENG

*A pagoda of puréed chestnuts smothered in vanilla cream
and decorated with preserved fruits*

Glazed Toffee Apples 186

BA TSU PING GUO

*Half a world away from fairground toffee apples, these
scrunchy prime apples are dunked in caramel and
showered with sesame seeds*

Glazed Toffee Bananas 186

BA TSU XIANG JIAO

. . . or bananas!

Fruit Mountain 188

SHI JIN SHUI GUO PAN

Generous chunks of seasonal fruit on a bed of ice

CONTENTS

INTRODUCTION

*E*ating out is something that most of us look forward to with pleasure and anticipation. It might be to celebrate some special occasion or event; it may even be an opportunity to give your loved one a chance to have a carefree night away from the kitchen stove. But we cannot always afford to eat out, and it is equally enjoyable to eat at home. So though cooking may not be one of your strong suits, for most of us there are those special occasions when you feel that you would like to spend time preparing that special Chinese something for someone you love. This then is the book for you.

When I was approached about this project I had just returned from several weeks in the East. My cup was brimming over with enthusiasm about the food and the culture! So, I agreed to write not only this book on Chinese Restaurant recipes, but a sister book on Thai recipes at the same time. An undertaking like this is a challenge I relish and in this I have been enormously well supported by my family, far beyond the call of duty.

During these past few months we have shared countless tasting sessions with enthusiastic food-loving friends and if their reactions are anything to go by you will not be disappointed in any of the recipes from either book.

May I thank you for buying this book. I hope that it will help and inspire you to try out recipes which you may have often thought you might cook but somehow you felt were too complicated or maybe had too many strange ingredients. These recipes fill in those gaps and the glossary completes the picture. Each recipe has been tried and tested, cooked stage by stage, so that your questions will be answered as you go along. It is a very practical book as you will find out and will add significantly to your culinary skills and confidence. I sincerely hope it will become one of the most popular books in your kitchen. I have certainly enjoyed researching, writing and cooking these recipes for you.

Now is the time to browse through the recipes and decide on a treat for your loved ones or plan for a special meal at the weekend. Go to it!

CHINESE FOOD AND
HOME COOKING

*T*here is no doubt that the Chinese are great culinary ambassadors, having taken their food to the furthest corners of the earth. Indeed, there can be very few towns anywhere which do not have at least one Chinese restaurant or takeaway, often more. Chinese food has ever been fresh, fast food; that, I suspect, is where its immense and long-lasting appeal lies.

Good food on the plate does not arrive there without considerable effort on the cook's part, no matter whether he or she is a beginner or an old hand. To the novice cook, the first essential is to realise that Chinese food will only be fast food when you have had some serious experience. You must allow time for the preliminary chopping and shredding and get into the habit of collecting all the different ingredients together *before* you start cooking, especially for stir-fry dishes.

The stir-fry method of cooking was born of necessity. The Chinese are inherently practical people. Over the centuries scarcity of fuel has meant that quick cooking was essential. Meat, poultry and fish used not to be plentiful either, and so the ingenious cooks evolved cooking methods and recipes to stretch those ingredients to the maximum. In these days of groaning super-market shelves, we can enjoy the clever combinations of fish and vegetables, poultry or meat and vegetables illustrated in delicious stir-fry recipes from the various regions of China without a thought to the meagre existence from which this cooking style evolved.

Ingredients for Chinese cooking are in the main familiar to us and easy to come by. The soy bean appears in a variety of guises and is especially valued for its high protein content. As light (thin) soy sauce and dark (thick) sauce it is used in hosts of dishes from stir-fries to the long-cook stews and soups for which the Chinese are famous, as well as the highly versatile beancurd and bean sprouts which we are using increasingly in our everyday cooking.

"Though you add a guest you needn't add another chicken" is a well-known Chinese proverb. Indeed, a clever Chinese cook or chef will create several different dishes from just one chicken or duck. Chicken, pork and duck are the most popular meats throughout China. In the north where wheat, maize and corn are grown, much more bread is eaten than rice. Noodles made from wheat are popular, and spaghetti can be used as a substitute. Lamb, mutton and beef are popular meats from the herds which graze the vast plains of the region.

Peking food, the sophisticated food of the emperors, is known as the Imperial cuisine. In China's capital this style of cooking has adopted and adapted many dishes brought by visitors and dignitaries from other regions over the centuries. This has resulted in an impressive range of cosmopolitan foods with the famous Peking duck surely being one of the most highly acclaimed dishes in the world.

Szechuan restaurants have great appeal for those of us who like hot and spicy dishes. This western area of China is spectacularly beautiful and crops such as wheat, corn, sugar cane, tea, cotton and citrus fruits grow in profusion. The cuisine is renowned for its generous use of hot peppers and frequently three flavours – hot, salt and sour – are combined in one dish. Typical Szechuan recipes are given on the following pages 85, 92, 118, 162, 170 and 179.

Though Pekingese and Szechuan restaurants are well represented in Britain, Cantonese restaurants are more common and this is because of mass emigration to other countries of South East Asia, Europe and America when times were very hard in the nineteenth century.

Food is very important to every Chinese and so wherever they went north, south, east or west they demanded their own particular cuisine. In true Chinese style the response to market forces resulted in the setting up of shops and restaurants.

The climate of the southern region is tropical with sugar and rice as the main crops and Cantonese cooking reflects these warmer climes. Citrus fruits, pineapples, bananas and lychees grow in abundance. Its extensive coastline provides an amazing selection of fish which are used widely in a wonderful selection of dishes. Some would say that Cantonese food is the best in China.

Stir-frying is especially popular with ginger, sugar, soy and oyster sauces giving flavour. Often the juices are lightly thickened with cornflour which gives a wonderful glossy finish to the lightly cooked foods. Sweet and sour, chicken and fish dishes are typical Cantonese fare as well as the snacks 'dim sum'. Many restaurants specialise in serving these little mouthfuls from a trolley throughout the day, but rarely are they served in the evening, which always seems a shame to me as they are quite delicious. They are, however, a real labour of love and apart from trying to cook one or two for the experience I would recommend that you go along to the restaurants which specialise in dim sum and marvel at the handiwork of the specialist dim sum chefs.

When I was approached to write this book I first made a collection of Chinese restaurant menus from all over Britain with the help of many friends. This enabled me to identify the most popular dishes on these menus from restaurants representing the different areas of China. I had generous help from a number of restaurants who gave me recipes for some of their most popular dishes. These were the Oriental Restaurant at the Dorchester, Joy King Lau in Chinatown and the Kaifeng Restaurant in North London, as well as the Panda in Soho, and I would like to thank them most warmly. Their addresses are on page 189.

Deh Ta Hsiung is a name you may be familiar with. He is a famous author and chef whom I have known for a number of years. He has been an enormous help to me at different stages of this book and especially for the translation of the recipe titles into Mandarin. For this I am most grateful.

I hope that my choice of Chinese Restaurant Menu Recipes includes a good number of your favourite dishes and that you will have as much fun as I have had in preparing and cooking them for friends. To me, the sharing of food round the table is truly one of life's real pleasures.

HOME COOKING

Stir-frying

No matter what is being cooked, all the ingredients must be ready before you start cooking, as the whole process is essentially fast in order to retain maximum flavour, colour and crispness, especially where vegetables are concerned. When all the ingredients are ready, warm the wok over a gentle flame then pour in the oil and swirl round before adding the first ingredients. When stir-frying you must keep everything on the move all the time to ensure even cooking.

Deep-frying

The wok is ideal for deep-frying, requiring less oil than conventional deep-frying pans yet providing a larger surface area for cooking. Use a thermometer to keep an eye on the temperature if possible.

Steaming

The beauty of bamboo baskets stacking neatly on top of each other is that they give great versatility. You can use just one basket or several over the same wok.

THE CHINESE KITCHEN –
BASIC EQUIPMENT FOR SUCCESS

*S*implicity is the key to the equipment required in the oriental kitchen. You will not need to spend vast amounts of money, but on the other hand do not go for the first wok, cleaver or steamer you happen to see as they vary enormously in quality and often in price too.

THE WOK

These wide, circular pans have a curved base which not only allows a large quantity of food to be cooked simultaneously over a large surface area but also allows for the evaporation of liquid essential in many recipes. It is the ideal shape for tossing food in stir-fry recipes and a much more satisfactory shape for deep-frying. There are many different qualities of wok on sale these days and the best advice is to go for the heaviest quality you can find, as the very thin, lightweight woks are a waste of time and money. This type will burn food very easily, which is bound to destroy your confidence in cooking oriental food.

I like to serve food straight from the wok. I have three cast-iron woks which I bought in Malaysia and they have built up a dark, glossy, black surface which shows off food to great advantage. I am completely sold on the wok as an essential piece of kitchen equipment. It can be used not only for stir-frying but for deep-frying and steaming as well as for non-oriental cooking, which is why my woks have pride of place next to the cooker where they are always ready for action.

I have a gas cooker, so I use metal stands on which the woks sit firmly during cooking. These are usually sold at the same time as the wok. For those with electric cookers there are Teflon-coated models with a flat base, or plug-in electric woks which you might consider. If you are not sure, ask for advice in a kitchen shop or try to watch a demonstration or even borrow one from a friend before you buy so that you choose the best for your needs.

Season your wok in the same way as a frying pan. Melt a little pure oil in the pan, swirl it round and leave over a very gentle heat for ten minutes. Cool it a little, empty out any excess, then rub vigorously with a pad of kitchen paper. This can be repeated regularly to build up a 'surface' on the wok, which over the years becomes truly 'non-stick'. Immediately after use, wash quickly in warm soapy water with a brush (do not use metal abrasive pads), then rinse, dry and brush over the cooking surface with oil.

A useful tip I learned from Ah Moi, our amah, was to warm the wok over a gentle heat before adding the oil for cooking. The oil then floods over the surface more easily and prevents food sticking. The amount of oil needed when cooking in a wok is considerably less than the amount you would use in a conventional pan, which must be a plus point in these health-conscious times.

THE SLICE

A wide-mouthed spatula is a perfect shape for stir-frying to keep the food on the move in the wok. A wooden spatula is usually recommended for the Teflon-surfaced woks.

CHOPPING BOARD

The oriental version looks like a huge slice of tree trunk, which is precisely what it is. They can be several centimetres thick and are very heavy in order to withstand all the chopping and slicing which is so much a part of food preparation.

CLEAVER

A multi-purpose, heavy, broad-bladed implement, the cleaver is used with such skill by oriental cooks for chopping, slicing, mincing, or even crushing a peeled clove of garlic by simply pressing down on the broad side of the blade. Ginger and lemon grass can be bruised in the same way.

PESTLE AND MORTAR, FOOD PROCESSOR AND COFFEE GRINDER

The pestle and mortar and/or food processor feature a great deal in this book.

The food processor makes everything possible for me and I really do recommend that you use one where appropriate in the recipes in this book. My Magimix is the next best thing to having a helper in the kitchen. The various blade attachments are invaluable where thin, even slices of onion, cucumber and similar are required.

A small coffee grinder can be a great help where small quantities of spices are to be ground but it is advisable that it is kept exclusively for this purpose.

STEAMERS

Bamboo, stacking-type steamers are available in a host of sizes from a wide range of stores. When not in use they look very attractive on a shelf in the kitchen, and I use my rather large versions as fruit baskets. Like all utensils in the oriental kitchen, they are multi-purpose. Indeed, the baskets can be used for serving as well as cooking the food. Where small items are being cooked, line the baskets with a piece of rinsed muslin. Several baskets can be stacked one on top of the other with the lid set on top. These are then set over the wok and the boiling water replenished as required. I have a metal trivet which sits in the wok over the water and enables me to cook, say, a whole fish in a large dish. Cover with a lid and keep an eye on the water level whilst steaming.

RICE COOKER

These are immensely popular and you can see why when up to three meals a day can be rice-based. The great advantage of the rice cooker is that it is foolproof and will happily keep the rice warm for up to five hours. Leftover rice can be reheated the following day and the cooker may also be used for steaming many dishes. (See page 38 on cooking rice.)

KNIVES

Last, but by no means least, I would like to stress the importance of a good set of knives. In the right hands, the cleaver covers all the chopping and slic-ing functions, but for those who do not have these skills then a well-balanced, stainless steel knife is a must. Good knives are not cheap but are a marvellous investment for any cook.

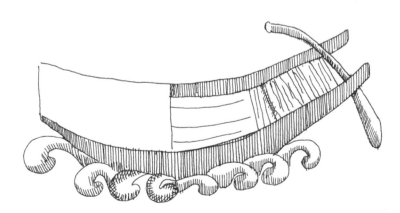

Glossary of Ingredients

 guide to some of the ingredients used in the book.

Bamboo Shoots
Large and smaller cans are widely available. The bamboo is either in whole pieces or sliced or shredded. Once opened, keep the bamboo shoots in the refrigerator. Cover with fresh cold water daily. Use within 7 days.

Beancurd
Essential in vegetarian cooking because of its high protein content, bean-curd (often called by the Japanese name 'tofu') has a smooth, baked custard-like texture with little flavour. It is best cooked with spicy or richly flavoured vegetables. Sold fresh in 7.5 cm/3 in square cakes for convenience, it is made from setting a liquid of ground soy bean with gypsum. Store fresh for up to 3 days in the refrigerator and change the water daily. A longlife version is also available. Refrigerate when opened and use as fresh.

Beans and Bean Paste

Black Beans
Salted, whole black beans are available in cans or jars. They should be rinsed to remove excessive saltiness before crushing. Refrigerate any leftover beans in a covered plastic or glass container and they'll keep well for several weeks. Or buy the ready crushed beans sold as black bean sauce.

Yellow Beans
Sold whole in cans or jars, crush the whole beans lightly before adding to the recipe; there is no need to rinse. Store as above. They are also available as a yellow bean sauce where less texture is required.

Hoisin or Barbecue Sauce
This is made from soy beans, garlic and spices. Used as a dip for spring rolls and to smear on pancakes for Peking duck or Kaifeng lamb (see pages 98 and 143). Also used as an ingredient in marinades, it is sold in jars and cans. It keeps well if covered and refrigerated after opening.

Bean Sprouts
These are usually the young sprout of the green mung bean, though in Asia

the larger soy bean is also sprouted, and are available in supermarkets and vegetable shops almost everywhere. They make an attractive addition to salads and stir-fry vegetables. They add bulk and crispness to spring rolls (see page 42). They will keep for 2–3 days in the refrigerator if covered in cold water which should be changed daily.

Chayote (Fat Sau Gwa)

This looks like a pale green avocado. It is a member of the squash family with a flat seed in the centre rather than a stone, which is discarded. Its crisp texture gives an interesting addition to stir-fry dishes. If you cannot find it, use peeled and deseeded cucumber.

Chillies

Red chillies are finger-like in shape. Green chillies are usually a little shorter but no less pungent. Treat both with respect in preparation. Open them up under running water to prevent the irritating oils getting near lips or eyes. Use rubber gloves or wash hands thoroughly with soap and water after preparation. Discard the seeds unless you like food very hot.

Dried chillies are often used. Break them into small pieces and discard the seeds. Soak to soften before pounding for some recipes.

Ready-prepared chopped chilli is widely available. Store in a cool dark place or in the refrigerator once opened.

Chinese Mushrooms

Good quality mushrooms may seem very expensive but you need relatively few to add their distinctive flavour to a wide variety of dishes. Soak for up to 30 minutes before using to soften them. Discard the tough stem and use the mushrooms either whole or in slices. Use the soaking liquid as a stock if required in the recipe or add to soups.

Chinese Rice Wine

A pale amber coloured wine which can be substituted for dry sherry.

Chinese Sausages

Lap cheong are dried, rather gnarled-looking sausages which have a chunkier filling than Western sausages. Steam them for 10 minutes until the skin plumps again. Cool then slice before adding to dishes like fried rice. They are available in most Chinese stores and supermarkets.

Cloud Ears and Wood Ears

These crinkly black fungi are appropriately named because of their 'cloud shape'. They are sold dried in boxes and have to be soaked for 30 minutes before using. They have no real flavour but add texture and crunch. Wood ears are much more common and also require soaking before use. The black, crinkly texture is striking when added to a range of dishes.

Coriander or Chinese Parsley

Sold with roots intact in large bunches in most Indian and oriental stores and in smaller bunches in supermarkets, this herb will keep well if washed and placed in a jug with 5 cm/2 in of water, changed daily. Cover the leaves with a plastic bag and keep in the refrigerator for up to a week. The leaves are used extensively all over the East as an ingredient and garnish.

Dried Prawns or Shrimps

These are sun-dried and have a long shelf life. They are sold in small packs and need to be soaked in water till they plump up before either using whole or chopping before use. They are available in Chinese or oriental stores.

Dry-fry Spices

This process makes all the difference to the subtle taste of spices. Dry-fry in a frying pan or wok, turning all the time over a gentle heat, until they give off their special aroma. Grind and use at once.

Five-Spice Powder

In Chinese supermarkets this aroma seems to pervade. It is made up from ground star anise, cloves, cinnamon, fennel and Szechuan pepper. Buy in small quantities as it soon loses its pungency.

Garlic

The whole garlic is a bulb or corm and each section a clove. People who are addicted to it claim that it cleanses the blood and aids digestion. No home should be without garlic – it adds a new dimension to food of all kinds. A garlic press is an essential piece of equipment; to make it easier to clean, just trim off the root of the clove of garlic – do not peel – squeeze it in the garlic press and lift out the skin.

Ginger

Young ginger with its pale creamy root, delicate pink nodules and green tips can be bought all over the East. It is used finely chopped in many stir-fry and fish dishes, but does not impart the pungent, aromatic flavour of the older, silvery-brown-skinned type that we can buy readily in the UK. This older type, known as a hand, must be either peeled or scraped then sliced and either chopped or pounded before using.

Bruised ginger is suggested in some recipes. Peel or scrape then give a sharp blow with the end of a rolling pin or in a pestle and mortar. The piece will then release its juices during cooking and can be removed from the dish before serving. Ginger should be wrapped closely in newspaper and stored in the vegetable box at the base of the refrigerator.

Lily Buds, Dried

Also known as golden needles, soak for 30 minutes in warm water before using to give a delicate musky taste. Some cooks insist that they should be tied in a knot before adding to food, so that they can be easily removed before serving. They are available in Chinese or oriental stores.

Lotus Root

These tubular roots with several 'waists' are sold already cooked in cans and are widely available in oriental stores. The slices are very attractive served as a salad with a sesame oil dressing, or added to a vegetable dish.

NOODLES

(Follow packet directions but as a general guide prepare as follows.)

Egg Noodles (Mee)

Fresh, thick egg noodles must be stored in the refrigerator and used within 2 days. Pour boiling water over them, then drain well before using. Cook dried egg noodles in boiling water for 2–3 minutes for thin, 5 minutes for thicker ones. Drain and rinse with boiling water.

Kway Teow

Flat, wide strips of rice noodles, these can be cut to the required width. They are available fresh and sometimes contain tiny pieces of spring onion or dried prawn. Scald with boiling water once cut and drain before frying.

Wheat Noodles

Soak these for 10 minutes in water first then cook in boiling water. Allow 2–3 minutes for thin noodles and 3–4 minutes for thicker ones. When using wholewheat spaghetti as a substitute, follow the packet directions.

Oyster Sauce

This thick, brown sauce of varying quality is made basically from an extract of oysters, salt and also starches. It accentuates flavours and accompanies meat and vegetable dishes very successfully.

Peppercorns

The black peppercorn is the whole berry or fruit of the peppercorn vine, picked then simply dried in the sun. The peppercorn spikes are spread out on mats and are raked over from time to time with a wooden rake until they have dried completely. This process takes about a week depending on the time of year and sunshine. The spike stems are removed in the raking.

The white peppercorn is the inner core of the ripened fruit. The green peppercorn is thoroughly washed in water then left to soak in slow running water for about a week to rot the outer skin. The fruit is then trampled to remove the spikes and bruise the soft skins. The final removal of the skins is done by washing and rubbing the peppercorns by hand in a sieve. The resulting white peppercorns are dried in the sun for a few days.

RICE

Rice is the staple food for two-thirds of the world's population. Thai jasmine rice is widely available and has a high reputation for quality and fragrance as it cooks. Many homes where rice is consumed in large quantities now have a rice cooker. If you do not have one, use the following method.

Plain Boiled Rice

Wash 225 g/8 oz/1 cup Thai jasmine rice thoroughly in several changes of water till the water looks clear. Place in a pan with 500 ml/17 fl oz/2¼ cups of water and bring to the boil. Reduce the heat, stir, cover the pan with a well-fitting lid and cook gently for 12–15 minutes. Remove the lid and stir with a chopstick or roasting fork so you do not break up the grains. Use at once or remove from the heat, clamp on the lid and enclose the pan in a sleeping bag or blanket. In this way the rice will keep warm for at least 1½–2 hours.

Microwave-cooked rice is very successful. Wash as above but cook the Thai jasmine rice in 450 ml/¾ pt/2 cups of boiling water in a large bowl three-quarters covered with clingfilm for 10 minutes on full power and 5 minutes resting in the microwave. Take out and stir as above.

For easy-cook rice, follow the packet directions.

Rice Wine Vinegar

A mild vinegar which I like to use in oriental cooking, you can use white wine or cider vinegar if not available.

Soy Sauce

An indispensable ingredient in the cooking of the East, thin soy sauce is commonly known as light sauce and is the most frequently used; the thick soy sauce is called dark sauce. The latter is stronger in flavour and should be used judiciously. Both are made from salted soya beans.

Star Anise

Use ground in five-spice powder, this is a very attractive, round, star shape with eight sections, which can all be used separately.

Straw Mushrooms

These are available in cans. Button mushrooms can be used as a substitute.

Szechuan Peppercorns

These are different from black peppercorns. For best results, they must be dry-fried before coarsely grinding and using in recipes. They are sometimes known as Chinese brown peppercorns and there is no substitute.

Tangerine Peel

This adds another dimension to chicken or duck dishes. Soak the small pieces for about 30 minutes before cooking. You can make your own by drying tangerine peel in a low oven. Store in an airtight container.

EATING CHINESE STYLE

*M*ost restaurants take the precaution of suggesting a series of set menus, some more elaborate than others, in order to make life easier for their uninitiated customers. These menus will usually feature a starter or platter of little snacks followed by a series of dishes featuring a variety of foods from fish to meat to noodles and rice with emphasis on colour, texture and flavours.

There is no way that you could, or even want to, emulate a full blown Chinese banquet at home, but there is a lot of fun to be had in cooking the odd recipe from this book as a supper dish and then when you have a few friends round perhaps cooking two or three favourite dishes from your repertoire to show off your new found skills.

Most of the recipes in this book serve three to four and more as part of a meal. As a rough guide, if you were cooking for six I suggest that you cook two dishes plus rice, with a stir-fry vegetable plus a soup and maybe a starter if you are well organised. Your guests will not only be impressed but will feel truly content.

Usually tea is drunk before and after the meal in China, with soup being drunk during the meal. However, the Chinese are not hidebound by form on this and will happily serve tea with the meal if you ask for it.

I like to serve glasses of rather weak tea throughout the meal which is greatly enjoyed by most of our guests. This is especially welcome when they get up clear headed the next morning! Try Jasmine, Oolong or Keemun tea to start with as they have rather delicate yet distinctive flavours and complement Chinese foods handsomely.

APPETISERS

PRAWN AND CRISPY NOODLE BALLS

XIA MEIN WAN ZI

The crispy noodle coating is made by crushing a few rice noodles (beehoon) in a plastic bag till they are a little larger than rice grains. They puff up when fried to give a rather attractive finish. Sesame seeds can be substituted.

Makes 20–24

225 g	uncooked prawns (shrimp), thawed if frozen	8 oz
2.5 ml	sugar	½ tsp
175 g	cod or haddock fillet, skinned and boned	6 oz
50 g	pork fat	2 oz
1 cm	fresh ginger, peeled and sliced	½ in
	Salt and freshly ground black pepper	
	A little beaten egg white	
150 g	rice noodles, crushed OR	5 oz
50 g	sesame seeds	2 oz
	Oil for deep-frying	
	Dipping sauce (see page 42)	

1. Place the prawns, sugar, fish, pork fat and ginger in a food processor and blend briefly. Season to taste.

2. Add sufficient egg white to form a paste and chill in the freezer for 15 minutes.

3. Form into 20–24 even-sized balls and coat in crushed noodles or sesame seeds.

4. Fry in hot oil at 190°C/375°F for 3–4 minutes until cooked through and the noodles are puffy and golden.

5. Serve with the same dipping sauce as the spring rolls.

CRISPY SHANGHAI SPRING ROLLS

CUI PI SHANGHAI CHUN JUAN

The skins or wrappers can be bought either in round or square shapes. If frozen, allow to thaw at room temperature. Open the parcel and using a palette knife separate the wrappers. Keep the pile of wrappers covered with a slightly damp cloth to prevent drying out before filling.

Makes 12

	FILLING:	
	6 Chinese mushrooms, soaked in water for 30 minutes	
350 g	beancurd	12 oz
225 g	finely minced (ground) pork	8 oz
30 ml	sunflower oil for frying	2 tbsp
225 g	cooked prawns (shrimp), chopped	8 oz
2.5 ml	cornflour (cornstarch)	½ tsp
15 ml	light soy sauce	1 tbsp
75 g	bamboo shoots, shredded	3 oz
75 g	water chestnuts, shredded	3 oz
75 g	bean sprouts	3 oz
	6 spring onions (scallions) or 1 young leek, finely chopped	
	A little sesame oil	
30 ml	plain (all-purpose) flour, mixed to a paste with water	2 tbsp
	12 spring roll wrappers, separated	
	Fat for deep-frying	
	DIPPING SAUCE:	
100 ml	light soy sauce	3½ fl oz/6½ tbsp
15 ml	chilli sauce or finely chopped fresh chilli	1 tbsp
	A little sesame oil	
	Rice vinegar to taste	

1. Drain the mushrooms, discard the stalks and slice the mushrooms finely. Cut the beancurd into similar-sized pieces.

2. Fry the pork in hot oil for 2–3 minutes, stirring all the time until the colour changes. Add the prawns.

3. Blend the cornflour and soy sauce, stir into the pork mixture then add the shredded bamboo shoots and water chestnuts.

4. Increase the heat, add the bean sprouts and spring onion or leek and toss constantly.

5. Add the mushroom slices and beancurd. Remove from the heat.

6. Taste for seasoning, stir in the sesame oil then allow to cool.

7. Make a paste from the flour and water.

8. Place a wrapper in a diamond shape in front of you. Spoon some of the filling near the centre and fold the nearest corner over the filling. Smear a little of the paste on the free sides.

9. Turn the sides to the middle and then continue to roll up. Repeat with remaining wrappers and filling. Place in a single layer on a baking tray lightly dusted with flour or cornflour.

10. Deep-fry in batches in hot oil at 190°C/375°F till crisp and golden then drain well on kitchen paper.

11. Serve at once with the dipping sauce made by mixing the soy, chilli sauce or fresh chilli and sesame oil together. Sharpen with a little vinegar, if liked.

VEGETARIAN SPRING ROLLS

SHU CHUN JUAN

Omit the pork and prawns for real vegetarians. Make in exactly the same way as above but first fry 1 large finely chopped onion with 1 cm/½ in peeled and finely shredded ginger. Add 1 peeled and grated carrot at the same time as the bean sprouts to give additional colour and flavour to the filling.

FRIED CRISPY WONTONS WITH APRICOT DIPPING SAUCE

GUO ZHI ZHA WON TON

These delicious little mouthfuls are a perfect starter or party snack. They are best served soon after cooking when they are warm and crisp. Make double quantity and freeze half to serve on another occasion which calls for 'a little something'. Fry from frozen, allowing an extra minute or so on the cooking time.

Makes about 24

24 wonton wrappers (about 50 g/2 oz)		
Oil for deep-frying		
FILLING:		
175 g	belly pork with a good balance of fat to lean	6 oz
100 g	prawns (shrimp) or cleaned and sliced squid	4 oz
2 spring onions (scallions), chopped		
10 ml	oyster sauce	2 tsp
Salt and freshly ground black pepper		
SPICY APRICOT SAUCE:		
225 g	apricot jam	8 oz
45 ml	cider or wine vinegar	3 tbsp
15 ml	warm water	1 tbsp
A little chilli sauce (optional)		

1. Do not take the wrappers out of the packet until you are ready to fill. Pour the oil into the pan.

2. Blend the pork, prawns or squid, spring onions, oyster sauce and seasoning to a paste in a food processor.

3. Place the wrappers singly on a clean worktop, 10 at a time, leaving the rest covered.

4. Place a tiny spoonful of the filling on to the centre of each wrapper. Damp two edges and fold over to form a triangle with the edges slightly off centre.

5. Now place two tiny blobs of the filling either side of the mound. Draw the points of the triangle over the filling and press down. The wings will then fall back. Repeat with the remaining filling and wrappers.

6. Place in a single layer on a lightly floured tray, cover with clingfilm and refrigerate if liked for several hours.

7. Prepare the sauce in advance. It can be reheated when required. Heat the jam, vinegar and water gently in a pan or in a microwave, stirring frequently until melted. For a smoother sauce push through a nylon sieve. Add chilli sauce if using. Pour into a bowl.

8. Heat oil to 190°C/375°F and cook the wonton in batches of 6 for 1–2 minutes, turning once. Drain on kitchen paper. Serve on a platter with the bowl of sauce in the centre for dipping.

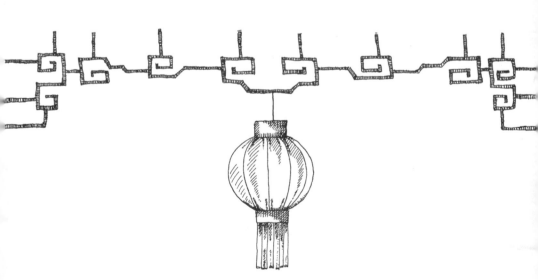

SALT AND PEPPER PRAWNS

JIAO YAN XIA

*T*his condiment is sometimes known as 'fried salt' or 'Cantonese salt'. It is made by dry-frying 10 ml/2 tsp of salt with 5 ml/1 tsp of Szechuan peppercorns over a medium heat till the peppercorns begin to release their flavour. Cool the mixture then crush in a pestle and mortar. Use as a table condiment or as a dip for deep-fried or roasted food or as an ingredient, as in this recipe. Black or white peppercorns can be substituted for the Szechuan peppercorns.

Serves 3–4 or 6 if part of a meal

450 g	large uncooked prawns (shrimp), about 18	1 lb
	Salt and pepper mix (see above)	
	3 shallots or 1 tiny onion, very finely chopped	
	2 cloves garlic, crushed	
1 cm	fresh ginger, peeled and very finely shredded	½ in
	1–2 red chillies, deseeded and thinly sliced	
2.5 ml	sugar or to taste	½ tsp
	3–4 spring onions (scallions), shredded	
	Oil for deep-frying	

1. Remove the heads and legs from prawns but leave on the body shell and tail. Dry on kitchen paper. Set aside with the prepared salt and pepper mix.

2. Prepare the onion, garlic, ginger and chillies and place on a large plate. Prepare the spring onions for garnish.

3. Heat the oil to 190°/375°F and fry the prawns for 1 minute then lift out and drain thoroughly.

4. Carefully pour away all except 30 ml/2 tbsp of the oil from the wok or spoon into a frying pan.

5. Reheat the oil then add the salt and pepper mix and the other ingredients plus the sugar and toss together for 1 minute.

6. Return the prawns to the mixture and toss together for a further minute till the shells of the prawns are impregnated with the seasonings.

7. Serve at once, garnished with spring onions.

CRISPY FRIED SEAWEED

CAI SUNG

*C*hoose rich coloured spring cabbage for this recipe. The leaves must be shredded as finely as possible then washed and left to dry for several hours so that the cabbage is completely dry before frying.
  Serves 6

350 g	spring greens	12 oz
	Oil for deep-frying	
	Salt and freshly ground black pepper	
	A little sugar	
	Toasted sesame seeds	

1. Shred the cabbage leaves as finely as possible. Discard the core and any thick stems. Drain and dry as suggested above.

2. Heat the oil to 190°/375°F just before the 'seaweed' is required. Use a frying basket if you have one so that the cabbage can be removed quickly from the hot oil once it is crisp. Cook in batches depending on the size of the pan. Allow about 2 minutes to fry and crisp.

3. Drain on kitchen paper.

4. Season to taste and sprinkle with a little sugar. Turn on to a serving plate.

5. Scatter with sesame seeds and serve at once.

STEAMED MUSSELS WITH BLACK BEAN SAUCE

SI ZHI QING TAI BEI

The scraping and cleaning of the mussels before the cooking is no longer such a tedious task. Farmed mussels from North Wales, Norfolk and Scotland are relatively free of barnacles. They are sold in 2 kg/4 lb bags which should serve at least 6 as a starter or 3–4 as a main course. For the very best results, prepare all the ingredients then cook whilst your family or guests sit and wait for this delicious dish. It tastes particularly good served with Steamed Flower Rolls (see page 60).

Serves 6 as a starter or 3–4 for lunch

2 kg	mussels	4 lb
	1 small onion, chopped	
60 ml	sunflower oil	4 tbsp
45 ml	rice wine or dry sherry	3 tbsp
450 ml	water	¾ pt/2 cups
1 cm	fresh ginger, peeled and shredded	½ in
	3 garlic cloves, crushed	
45 ml	salted black beans, rinsed and lightly crushed	3 tbsp
30 ml	oyster sauce	2 tbsp
	A little brown sugar	
	Salt and freshly ground black pepper	
	4 spring onions (scallions), thinly shredded	

1. Scrape any barnacles from the shells of the mussels with a sharp knife and remove the 'beard', the device which the mussel uses to attach itself to the rock or breeding platform. Wash several times in fresh water and leave covered with water in a cool place until required.

2. When all the other ingredients and your guests are ready, fry the onion in 30 ml/2 tbsp of the oil in a very large pan until soft. Add the rice wine or sherry and then the water and bring to the boil.

3. Toss in all the mussels, cover with a lid and shake the pan over a high heat for 4 minutes or until the mussels are open. Remove from the heat and pour the cooking liquid through a sieve. Reserve the liquid.

4. Heat the remaining oil in a wok, and fry the ginger and garlic without browning, stirring all the time, then add the beans, oyster sauce and 300 ml/½ pt/1¼ cups or more of the cooking liquid if you want a more soup-like sauce.

5. Cook for 1 minute, add the sugar and seasoning to taste then add all the mussels to the wok with half the spring onions.

6. Toss together for 1 minute before serving garnished with spring onion.

SUNSHINE AND SNOWFLAKE TOASTS

CHI MA XAI TU SSU

Use a three or four day old sliced loaf in this recipe as slightly stale bread will absorb less oil when frying. Trim the crusts from the prepared toasts and cut into triangles, squares or long finger shapes or prawn straws. You can prepare ahead and freeze then cook from frozen.
Makes 4 slices, cuts into 24 pieces

225 g	frozen prawns (shrimp), thawed	8 oz
50 g	pork fat	2 oz
1 cm	fresh ginger, peeled and sliced	½ in
	1 clove garlic, crushed	
	6 water chestnuts from a 550 g/1¼ lb can	
5 ml	dry sherry	1 tsp
5 ml	cornflour (cornstarch)	1 tsp
	A little egg white	
	Salt and freshly ground black pepper	
	4 slices bread	
25 g	sesame seeds	1 oz
	Oil for deep-frying	
	Fresh coriander (cilantro) leaves to garnish	

1. Drain then dry the prawns on kitchen paper. Place in a food processor with the sliced pork fat, ginger, garlic and water chestnuts. Blend briefly to a paste. Add the sherry, cornflour and sufficient egg white to bind the mixture. Season to taste.

2. Turn into a bowl. Spread the paste on to one side of the bread slices only and press sesame seeds on to the paste. Trim the crusts and cut into shapes.

3. Heat the oil to 190°C/375°F and fry the toasts paste-side down for 3 minutes then flip over and fry for a further 2 minutes. Drain on kitchen paper and serve at once garnished with coriander leaves. Serve with Crispy Fried Seaweed (see page 47).

BARBECUED PORK SPARERIBS

MI ZHI SHAO PAI GU

Select even-sized meaty ribs for even cooking. Allow to marinate in the spicy sauce for at least 2 hours. Cook in the oven, then transfer to the barbecue for the last few minutes if you like.

Serves 3–4 or more if part of a meal

1 kg	meaty spareribs	2¼ lb
	MARINADE:	
45 ml	soy sauce	3 tbsp
45 ml	hoisin sauce	3 tbsp
45 ml	Chinese wine or dry sherry	3 tbsp
25 g	dark brown sugar	1 oz
	1 clove garlic, crushed	
1 cm	fresh ginger, peeled and finely chopped	½ in
5 ml	five-spice powder	1 tsp
5 ml	salt	1 tsp

Shredded lettuce leaves and spring onion
(scallion) tassels to garnish

1. Prick the meaty parts of the spareribs with a fork or skewer and arrange in a large shallow dish.

2. Heat the soy, hoisin and Chinese wine or sherry with the sugar until the sugar has dissolved. Add the garlic, ginger, five-spice powder and salt. Remove from the heat, cool slightly then pour over the ribs and leave to marinate for at least 2 hours.

3. Set the oven to 190°C/375°F/gas 5. Cook the ribs on a trivet over a foil-lined roasting tin for about 1 hour, basting twice with the remaining marinade.

4. When the spareribs are a rich mahogany colour and cooked through, serve hot on a platter with shredded lettuce and garnished with spring onion tassels.

LETTUCE PARCELS

SHENG CAI BAO

This is what we now refer to as an activity meal! The filling with a whole range of different textures and flavours can be served warm or cold in one of nature's wrappings: a simple crisp lettuce leaf. If you prefer you could use the same quantities of finely chopped chicken breast and prawns instead of the pork. It can be fun to take on a picnic too.
    Serves 4–6

225 g	French beans, cut into 2.5 cm/1 in lengths	8 oz
75–90 ml	sunflower oil	5–6 tbsp
1 cm	fresh ginger, peeled and shredded	½ in
	2 garlic cloves, crushed	
450 g	pork, finely minced (ground)	1 lb
30 ml	rice wine or dry sherry	2 tbsp
30–45 ml	chicken stock or water	2–3 tbsp
100 g	canned bamboo shoots, sliced and shredded	4 oz
	12 water chestnuts, coarsely chopped	
100 g	salted peanuts, lightly crushed	4 oz
30 ml	oyster sauce	2 tbsp
	A little sugar	
	Salt and freshly ground black pepper	
10 ml	sesame oil	2 tsp
	A few fresh coriander (cilantro) leaves, chopped	
	TO SERVE:	
	Leaves from a large iceberg lettuce	
100 ml	hoisin sauce	3½ fl oz/6½ tbsp

1. Blanch the beans in boiling water for 1 minute. Refresh in cold water, then drain and reserve.

2. Heat the wok then spoon in 30 ml/2 tbsp of the oil and when hot fry the ginger and garlic without browning for 30 seconds.

3. Add the pork and stir-fry for 4 minutes until the meat changes colour. Add the rice wine or sherry then transfer to a bowl.

4. Add the remaining oil to the wok and fry the beans for 1 minute. Add the stock or water and cook for 2 minutes then add the bamboo shoots and water chestnuts, stirring all the time.

5. Now add peanuts, oyster sauce, reserved pork mixture, sugar and seasoning. Cook gently for 3–4 minutes.

6. Remove from the heat and stir in the sesame oil and chopped coriander leaves. Turn into a serving bowl.

7. Arrange the washed and dried lettuce leaves on serving platter and pour the hoisin sauce into a small bowl.

8. Guests spoon some of the filling on to each lettuce leaf, roll up into a neat parcel and dip in hoisin sauce before eating.

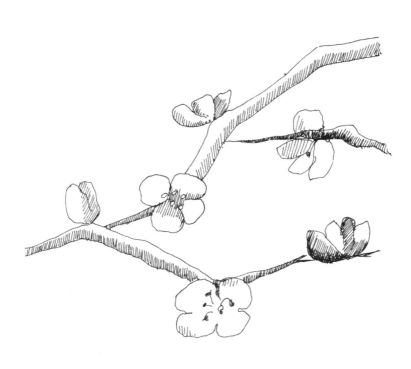

SCRAMBLED EGGS WITH MUSHROOMS IN PANCAKES

MU HSU ROU

nother interesting filling in a parcel, this time using the well-known Mandarin pancakes. These pancakes, about 10 in a pack, can be bought from oriental stores and major supermarkets. They should be reheated by steaming for 2–3 minutes or in the microwave for 15 seconds. Reheat when everyone is ready to eat, so that they are warm and pliable. I like to serve sliced cucumber along with the pancakes to give an extra dimension in texture and flavour.

Serves 4 for lunch or 8 as a starter

	6 dried Chinese mushrooms, soaked in water for 30 minutes	
15 ml	dark soy sauce (optional)	1 tbsp
15 ml	rice wine or dry sherry	1 tbsp
	Freshly ground black pepper	
	2–3 spring onions (scallions), finely shredded	
100 g	lean pork, cut into fine strips	4 oz
100 g	bamboo shoots, cut into fine shreds	4 oz
30–45 ml	groundnut (peanut) oil	2–3 tbsp
1 cm	fresh ginger, peeled and shredded	½ in
	4 eggs, beaten	
	Dash of sesame oil	
	1–2 packs of Mandarin pancakes	
	½ cucumber, sliced or cut into fingers	

1. Drain the mushrooms, discard the stalks and slice caps finely.

2. Blend the soy sauce, if using, with the rice wine or sherry, pepper and spring onions.

3. Prepare the pork and bamboo shoots.

4. Heat a wok, add 15 ml/1 tbsp of the oil and when hot fry the ginger for 30 seconds without browning. Add the beaten eggs and scramble them until just firm. Lift out and break up with a slice. This could be done in a separate non-stick pan.

5. Clean the wok and heat the remaining oil. Add the pork and fry briskly for 1–2 minutes until it changes colour. Add the bamboo shoots, mushroom and spring onion mixture.

6. Toss continuously for 1 minute then add the scrambled egg mixture and toss again. Remove from the heat, add the sesame oil and taste for seasoning.

7. Heat the pancakes then place a spoonful of the mixture on to each one, roll up, tucking in the sides as you roll and eat at once with the pieces of cucumber.

CANTONESE EGG FOO YUNG

SHI JIN FU RON

A hearty omlette which can be either cooked as one large omelette and divided into portions, or the mixture used to cook the omelettes individually. Either way it can be a vehicle to use up a variety of leftovers from cooked ham, chicken, pork, vegetables, seafood or what you will.

Serves 3–4 or more as part of a meal

	6 Chinese mushrooms, soaked in warm water for 30 minutes	
50 g	roast pork, cut into fine shreds	2 oz
50 g	bean sprouts	2 oz
	6 water chestnuts, chopped	
	3 Chinese leaves or 50 g/2 oz spinach leaves, washed and finely shredded	
60 ml	sunflower oil	4 tbsp
	4 eggs, beaten	
	Salt and freshly ground black pepper	
2.5 ml	sugar	½ tsp
5 ml	rice wine or dry sherry	1 tsp

1. Drain the mushrooms, discard the stalks and slice the caps thinly.

2. Prepare the pork, bean sprouts, water chestnuts and Chinese leaves or spinach. Have the remaining ingredients to hand.

3. Heat a frying pan (skillet), add half the oil then toss in the pork and vegetables, stirring for 1 minute.

4. Add this mixture to the beaten eggs.

5. Clean the pan and reheat the remaining oil. Turn in the egg mixture. When the omelette has set on the underside, sprinkle with seasoning and sugar.

6. Turn on to a large plate and then invert the pan over the uncooked side so that the omelette can be cooked on the second side. Alternatively, cut in half and turn over with a large spatula.

7. Drizzle the rice wine or sherry over the omelette and serve immediately cut into wedges, or try serving cold wrapped in lettuce leaves for a picnic.

TEA EGGS

CH'A YEH TAN

So attractive and yet so simple! Just gently crack the shell of the boiled eggs without removing any of the shell then soak overnight in the spiced tea. When the eggs are eventually peeled just before serving they will have a 'crazed' effect which looks so pretty.

Makes 6

	6 eggs, gently boiled for 20 minutes	
30 ml	dark soy sauce	2 tbsp
5 ml	salt	1 tsp
	½ star anise	
	30 ml/2 tbsp tea or 2 teabags	

1. Allow the eggs to cool, then gently crack the egg shells leaving the shells intact.

2. Place eggs in a large pan of water with the soy sauce, salt, star anise and tea. Bring to the boil then simmer for 1 hour. Add more boiling water if necessary to ensure that the eggs remain covered.

3. Allow to cool in the water for several hours or overnight. Remove the shells just before serving cut into quarters as a starter.

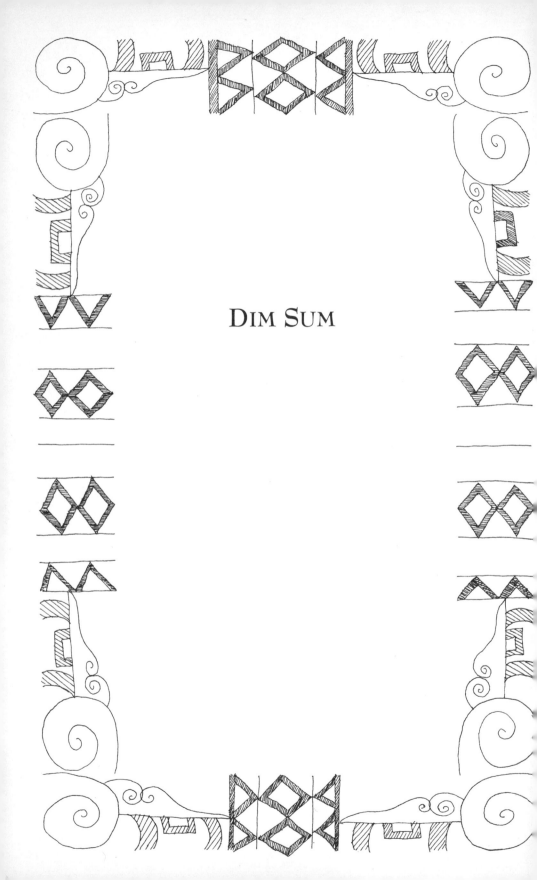

DIM SUM

BASIC DOUGH FOR STEAMED BUNS

DIM SUM

im Sum actually means 'touch of heart'. A selection of mouth-wateringly light buns to serve with a variety of dishes.
Makes 16

15 ml	sugar	3 tsp
(Use only 5 ml/1 tsp for Flower Rolls)		
300 ml (approx) warm water		½ pt/1¼ cups
depending on the flour used		
25 ml	dried yeast	1½ tbsp
450 g strong or plain (all-purpose) flour		1 lb
5 ml	salt	1 tsp
15 g	lard	½ oz/1 tbsp

1. Dissolve the sugar in half the water then sprinkle in the yeast. Stir and leave for 10–15 minutes until the mixture is frothy.

2. Meanwhile, sift the flour and salt together in a bowl and leave in a warm place or put into a food processor. Rub in lard or process briefly.

3. Stir in the yeast mixture with sufficient of the remaining water to make a soft but not too sticky dough.

4. Knead for 1 minute in the food processor or on a floured board by hand for 10 minutes.

5. Pop into a large oiled plastic bag, seal the top and leave in a warm place until it doubles in size.

6. Knock out any air bubbles and knead again for 5 minutes or 30 seconds in the food processor. Now make into one of the following.

STEAMED FLOWER ROLLS

HUA JUAN

This delicious recipe is traditionally served with Aromatic Crispy Duck (see page 100).
Makes 16

Basic Dough (see page 59)		
15 ml	sesame oil	1 tbsp

1. Divide the dough in half. Roll each piece into a rectangular shape, 30 x 20 cm/12 x 8 in.

2. Brush the surface of one rectangle with sesame oil and set the other piece on top.

3. Roll up like a Swiss roll, trim the ends and cut into 16 even pieces.

4. Take the 'rolls' one by one and press down firmly on the rolled side with a chopstick.

5. Now place the roll on the worktop, coiled side uppermost, and first pinch the opposite ends with fingers of both hands, and then pull the ends underneath to seal. The dough should separate into petals.

6. Place, sealed-side down, on lightly greased trays or on vegetable parchment paper that will fit into the steamer.

7. Allow them to rise until they are double in size, then steam over fast boiling water for 35 minutes.

STEAMED PORK BUNS

ROU BAOZI

*W*e would invariably oven-bake a yeast-type dough, but in China
few people have ovens so the buns are steamed which gives them
quite a different appearance. When cooked they have a soft, spongy
texture which is best eaten straight from the steamer. However, they can
be reheated satisfactorily in the steamer without spoiling.
Makes 16

Basic Dough (see page 59)		
FILLING:		
225 g	Roast Pork (see page 147)	8 oz
	A little oil for frying	
	1 garlic clove, crushed	
	2 spring onions (scallions), chopped	
10 ml	yellow bean sauce	2 tsp
10 ml	sugar	2 tsp
5 ml	cornflour (cornstarch) mixed to a paste with water	1 tsp

1. Prepare the dough. While it is rising for the first time prepare the filling.

2. Slice and then shred the pork into tiny pieces. Heat the wok, add the oil and when hot fry the garlic for a few seconds then add the pork, spring onions and yellow bean sauce. Add the sugar and thicken slightly with cornflour paste. Remove from the heat and cool.

3. Divide the dough into 16 pieces. Roll each piece into 7.5–10 cm/3–4 in rounds.

4. Place a spoonful of the filling into the centre of each piece of dough and gather up the sides into a purse shape to enclose the filling. Twist the top to seal.

5. Set the buns on tiny squares of vegetable parchment in a steamer and leave to double in size.

6. Steam over fast boiling water for 30–35 minutes until cooked through.

TURNIP PASTE SQUARES

LAW PAK GO

This was served to me at Joy King Lau, right in the heart of London's Chinatown. It is made from moolie, the oriental radish, which is now available even in our large supermarkets.

Serves 4

450 g	1 large moolie, peeled and coarsely grated	1 lb
100 g	plain (all-purpose) flour 4 oz/1 cup	
Salt and freshly ground black pepper		
1–2 Chinese sausage, steamed and chopped		
25 g	dried shrimp, soaked for 30 minutes and chopped	1 oz
Oil for shallow frying		

1. Place the moolie in boiling water to cover and cook for 30 minutes until tender. Drain very well. Make into a purée in a food processor.

2. Whilst still warm, add the flour and seasoning to make a thick batter. Stir in the chopped sausage and shrimp.

3. Pour into a dish 15 cm x 20 cm/6 in x 8 in and leave in freezer or the coldest part of the refrigerator to set.

4. Cut into neat squares and when the guests are ready just shallow-fry the squares on each side till golden and crisp.

STEAMED BUNS WITH PORK AND PRAWN STUFFING

SUI MAI

he pork and prawn combination is a classic. Serve these buns hot with one of the soy-based dips (page 64). Any leftovers can be frozen. Simply reheat by steaming over fast-boiling water for 10 minutes. Makes 16

Basic Dough (see page 59)		
FILLING:		
225 g	prawns (shrimp), fresh or thawed if frozen	8 oz
2.5 ml	sugar	½ tsp
175 g	pork, finely minced (ground)	6 oz
50 g	pork fat	2 oz
1 cm	fresh ginger, peeled and finely shredded	½ in
Salt and freshly ground black pepper		
A little beaten egg white to bind		

1. Prepare the dough. While it is rising for the first time prepare the filling.

2. Drain the prawns well if they have been frozen.

3. Place in a food processor with the sugar, pork, pork fat, ginger and seasoning then process briefly.

4. Add the lightly beaten egg white little by little until the mixture forms a paste. Place in the freezer for 15 minutes to chill thoroughly.

5. Divide the dough into 16 pieces. Roll each piece into 7.5–10 cm/3–4 in rounds.

6. Place a spoonful of the filling into the centre of each piece of dough and gather up the sides into a purse shape to enclose the filling. Twist the top to seal.

7. Set the buns on tiny squares of vegetable parchment in a steamer and leave to double in size.

8. Steam over fast boiling water for 30–35 minutes until cooked through.

DIPS OR SAUCES
TO SERVE WITH DIM SUM

SOY AND VINEGAR
JIANG CU YU

Blend 45 ml/3 tbsp of light soy sauce with 15 ml/1 tbsp of rice vinegar or red wine vinegar. Add a small deseeded and finely chopped chilli if liked.

SOY AND GARLIC
SUAN JIANG YU

Peel and crush 2 garlic cloves then blend with 45 ml/3 tbsp of light soy sauce, 15 ml/1 tbsp rice vinegar and a little sesame oil. Add a few toasted sesame seeds if liked.

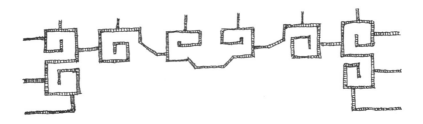

SOUPS

PORK BALL AND WATERCRESS SOUP

ROU WAN YANG CAI TANG

*C*ellophane noodles, sometimes called bean thread noodles, are made from soy beans. They are very clear, very fine and crystal-like. They need to be soaked briefly then cut into shorter lengths with scissors before quickly cooking in boiling water for 1–2 minutes. Drain and rinse with cold water. Finely minced lean beef can be used instead of pork if you prefer.

Serves 4–6

225 g	finely minced (ground) pork	8 oz
2.5 ml	sugar	½ tsp
15 ml	cornflour (cornstarch)	1 tbsp
5 ml	rice wine or dry sherry	1 tsp
	Salt and freshly ground black pepper	
	A little beaten egg	
1.5 litres	chicken stock	2½ pt/6 cups
25 g	cellophane or bean thread noodles, soaked	1 oz
	1 large bunch of watercress, washed and thick stems removed	

1. Blend the pork with the sugar, cornflour, rice wine or dry sherry and seasoning. Add sufficient beaten egg just to bind.

2. Form into 18 small balls then place on a lightly oiled plate and steam in a covered wok or deep frying pan for 20 minutes. Alternatively, the balls can be fried in a little oil for 10 minutes until cooked.

3. Allow the stock to come to the boil. Check for seasoning.

4. Cut the cellophane noodles into short lengths with scissors. Cover with boiling water and cook for 1 minute then drain and rinse.

5. Spoon some of the noodles, watercress and pork balls into bowls and ladle the hot, well flavoured stock on top.

PEKING DUCK SOUP
WITH THREE VEGETABLES

YA ROU SAN SI TANG

ypical of the 'waste not, want not' attitude of the ever-resourceful Chinese, this soup is made using the left over carcass of the Peking duck or Roast Honey Duck (see pages 98 and 111).
    Serves 4–5

	1 cooked duckling carcass, broken into small pieces	
1.5 litres	stock or water	2½ pt/6 cups
	4 celery sticks, chopped	
	3 leeks, sliced	
1 cm	fresh ginger, peeled and finely chopped	½ in
	Salt and freshly ground black pepper	
45 ml	light soy sauce	3 tbsp
5 ml	sugar	1 tsp
225 g	Chinese leaves, shredded	8 oz

1. Place the duck carcass pieces in a deep pan with the stock or water, celery, 2 of the leeks and the ginger.

2. Allow to come to the boil, then skim and add seasoning to taste. Simmer, half covered for 40 minutes.

3. Strain the stock into a clean pan, add the remaining shredded leek, the soy sauce and sugar.

4. Continue to simmer a further 10 minutes. Finally add the shredded Chinese leaves and cook for a further 2–3 minutes.

5. Taste for seasoning and serve in soup bowls or in a large tureen for guests to help themselves.

HOT AND SOUR SOUP

SUAN LA TANG

oups are an important part of a Chinese meal. This popular and substantial soup from Northern China would usually be served as a separate course rather than alongside other dishes. Wood ears, a dried fungus, and lily buds or golden needles, a dried flower stem, can also be used. Reconstitute them in the same way as the mushrooms. Use six pieces of each in this recipe.

Serves 6

4-6 Chinese dried mushrooms, soaked in warm water for 30 minutes		
6 small pieces wood ear and lily buds if using, soaked in water with the mushrooms		
175 g	fresh beancurd, drained	6 oz
100 g	pork fillet, cut into fine strips	4 oz
45 ml	cornflour (cornstarch)	3 tbsp
150 ml	water	¼ pt/⅔ cup
15-30 ml	sunflower oil	1-2 tbsp
1 small onion, finely chopped		
1.5 litres	beef or chicken stock or consommé	2½ pt/6 cups
60 ml	rice wine vinegar	4 tbsp
15 ml	light soy sauce	1 tbsp
Salt and freshly ground black pepper		
1 egg, beaten		
5 ml	sesame oil	1 tsp
2-3 spring onions (scallions), shredded		

1. Drain the soaking water from the mushrooms and reserve. Discard the stems and slice the caps finely. Drain the wood ears if using and trim away the tough stem, then cut into small pieces. Tie the lily buds into a knot.

2. Cut the beancurd into neat dice and set aside.

3. Dust the pork fillet pieces with a little of the cornflour and mix the remaining cornflour to a paste with water.

4. Heat the oil and fry the onion until soft. Increase the heat and fry the pork fillet until the pieces change colour.

5. Add the stock or consommé and the mushroom slices along with the reserved soaking water. Bring to the boil and simmer for 15 minutes.

6. Stir in the cornflour paste to thicken then add the beancurd, vinegar, soy sauce and seasoning.

7. Lower the heat and drizzle in the beaten egg from a whisk, or to be authentic the fingertips, so that it forms threads in the soup.

8. Add the sesame oil just before serving and garnish each helping with spring onion shreds.

WONTON SOUP

WONTON TANG

his clear soup, Cantonese in origin, features the tiny dumplings filled with a finely ground pork and ginger mixture. The small square wonton wrappers can be purchased from most oriental stores and supermarkets.

Serves 6

	18 wonton wrappers	
100 g	finely minced (ground) lean pork	4 oz
1 cm	ginger, peeled and finely chopped	½ in
15 ml	light soy sauce	1 tbsp
	Salt	
100 g	spinach leaves, washed and dried	4 oz
1.5 litres	chicken stock	2½ pt/6 cups
30 ml	rice wine or dry sherry	2 tbsp

1. If the wonton wrappers have been frozen, thaw then separate carefully. Leave them under a slightly damp cloth to prevent drying out while preparing the filling.

2. Mix the pork, ginger, soy sauce and salt together.

3. Place a tiny teaspoon of the filling on to the centre of each wonton positioned like a diamond in front of you.

4. Take the nearest point over the filling and tuck in. Roll up almost to the peak. Damp the edges slightly then pull the wings under the wonton to form a hat shape.

5. Repeat with the remaining wrappers and filling.

6. Remove the stems from the spinach leaves and tear into shreds.

7. Bring the stock to the boil. Add the wontons and cook for 3–5 minutes.

8. Just before serving add the spinach and cook for 1 minute. Add the rice wine or sherry and taste for seasoning. Serve hot.

CHICKEN AND SWEETCORN SOUP

JI TI YUMI TANG

F or the following three soups a really good quality stock is essential – a perfect item to have in the freezer which then means that these soups can be made in minutes.

Serves 6

100 g	boneless chicken breast	4 oz
45 ml	ice cold water	3 tbsp
15 ml	rice wine or dry sherry	1 tbsp
1.5 litres	chicken stock	2½ pt/6 cups
2.5 ml	sugar	½ tsp
400 g	can creamed sweetcorn	14 oz
30 ml	cornflour (cornstarch) mixed to a paste with water	2 tbsp
	Salt and freshly ground black pepper	
	1 egg white, lightly beaten	
	2 spring onions (scallions), finely shredded	

1. Mince the chicken breast with a very sharp knife then pound with the back of the knife until it's very smooth or pound in a food processor.

2. Remove any tendons, add the cold water and mix well. Pour off any water which has not been absorbed, stir in the wine or sherry. Set aside.

3. Bring the stock, sugar and sweetcorn to the boil in a pan. Add the cornflour paste and stir until the soup thickens slightly.

4. Lower the heat, taste for seasoning then stir in the chicken mixture and egg white and continue stirring for 2 minutes.

5. Serve in bowls garnished with the shredded spring onion.

BEANCURD SOUP WITH VARIATIONS

SHI JIN DAO FU TANG

resh beancurd can be kept covered with cold water for 2–3 days in the refrigerator but replace the water daily. A longlife version is also available which is a very useful addition to the store cupboard.
Serves 4

350 g	beancurd or longlife beancurd	12 oz
1.5 litres	vegetable or chicken stock	2½ pt/6 cups
	Salt and freshly ground black pepper	
	Shredded spring onion (scallion) or watercress leaves to garnish	

	VARIATIONS:	
	6 Chinese mushrooms, soaked in water for 30 minutes	
100 g	bean sprouts	4 oz
100 g	bamboo shoots, drained and cut into matchsticks	4 oz

1. Drain the beancurd and cut into neat dice.

2. Heat the stock and season to taste.

3. Prepare any of the variations you might be adding. If using the mushrooms, discard the tough stems, slice thinly and add to the stock, allowing to simmer for 15 minutes. The bean sprouts or the bamboo shoots need only be added at the last minute.

4. Just before serving, slip the diced beancurd into the pan and reheat gently with any of the variations for only 1–2 minutes.

5. Serve in bowls garnished with spring onion or watercress leaves.

EGG DROP SOUP WITH SPINACH

PO CAI DAN FUA TANG

real favourite which is found on most restaurant menus, this is simplicity itself to prepare, the flavour depending largely on the use of a really good stock. The beaten egg is added in a thin stream at the last minute and immediately forms attractive threads in the slightly thickened soup.

Serves 6

1.5 litres	good chicken, duck or vegetable stock	2½ pt/6 cups
Salt and freshly ground black pepper		
A few spinach leaves, torn into small pieces		
45 ml	cornflour (cornstarch) blended to a paste with 90 ml/6 tbsp cold water	3 tbsp
1 egg, beaten with 30 ml/2 tbsp cold water		

1. Bring the stock to the boil and assemble the other ingredients.

2. Add the spinach leaves and cook for only 1 minute, so that the leaves retain their colour.

3. Thicken with the blended cornflour then taste and adjust the seasoning.

4. Pour the egg mixture from a basin into the pan in a thin stream, stirring all the time.

5. Serve immediately in warmed bowls.

SEAFOOD

STIR-FRY SCALLOPS WITH MANGETOUT AND GARLIC

XUE DAO CHAO DAIZI

rozen scallops must be completely thawed and well dried on kitchen paper so that all the excess water is removed. Slice larger scallops into two rounds, removing the coral, but leave smaller scallops whole. Never overcook them otherwise they become tough.

Serves 3, or more as part of a buffet

450 g	scallops, thawed if frozen	1 lb
2.5 ml	sugar	½ tsp
	Freshly ground black pepper	
	3 garlic cloves, crushed	
45 ml	groundnut (peanut) oil or sunflower oil	3 tbsp
45 ml	rice wine or dry sherry	3 tbsp
15 ml	light soy sauce	1 tbsp
100 g	mangetout (snow peas)	4 oz
5 ml	cornflour (cornstarch) blended with water to a paste (optional)	1 tsp
5 ml	sesame oil	1 tsp
	Spring onion (scallion) curls	

1. Prepare the scallops, sprinkle with sugar and black pepper.

2. Prepare all the other ingredients. As with all stir-fry recipes, cook just before serving.

3. Fry the garlic in the hot oil but do not allow to brown. Quickly add the scallops and toss constantly for no longer than 2 minutes until opaque. Add the corals if cooking large scallops.

4. Add the rice wine or sherry and soy sauce and when bubbling add the mangetout. Keep tossing for 30 seconds and thicken the sauce with the cornflour paste if liked. Add more pepper to taste. Drizzle with sesame oil and garnish with spring onion curls.

BRAISED CARP

HONG SHAO LI YU

I have never forgotten being told that the cheek of the fish is the most prized morsel and is always therefore served to the most honoured guest! Even though carp are available all year round, best be on the safe side and order in advance. Ask the fishmonger to gut, scale and clean the fish, leaving on the head and tail which makes a more attractive presentation as well as being aesthetically correct.

Serves 4

	1 carp (1 kg/2¼ lb) cleaned and scaled, head and tail intact	
	Salt	
30 ml	cornflour (cornstarch)	2 tbsp
	Oil for deep-frying	
2.5 cm	fresh ginger, peeled and cut into shreds	1 in
	2 garlic cloves, crushed	
	6 spring onions (scallions), white part left whole and tops shredded	
30 ml	light soy sauce	2 tbsp
300 ml	fish or chicken stock	½ pt/1¼ cups
45 ml	rice wine or dry sherry	3 tbsp
	Freshly ground black pepper	
	1 red chilli, deseeded and finely shredded	
	Fresh coriander (cilantro) leaves to garnish	

1. Wash the carp and dry thoroughly with kitchen paper. Slash the flesh on each side of the fish two or three times. Dry thoroughly then rub with salt inside and out and then dust with half the cornflour to prevent sticking in the pan or wok.

2. Heat the oil in a large wok to 180°C/350°F. Either slide the fish gently into the hot oil or hold up by the tail and baste with the hot oil to seal the skin, then lower into the wok and cook for about 8 minutes depending on the size of the fish.

3. Lift carefully on to a tray lined with kitchen paper to drain. This can be done ahead of time and the fish left to rest until required.

4. Allow the oil to cool then drain off all but 45 ml/3 tbsp from the wok or spoon this oil into a separate large frying pan.

5. Fry the ginger, garlic and white parts of the spring onion in the oil without browning. Add the soy sauce and stock.

6. About 15 minutes before serving, gently place the fish in the hot sauce and cook until just tender. Baste frequently and be careful not to overcook.

7. Gently lift the fish on to a serving platter. Thicken the sauce with the remaining cornflour mixed to a paste with water. Add the rice wine or sherry and seasoning to taste.

8. Pour the sauce over the fish and garnish with the shredded spring onion tops, chilli and coriander leaves.

FRIED FISH WITH GREEN AND WHITE VEGETABLES

WU LIU YU

*I*n this recipe the fish fillets are first cut into thick finger-like pieces then marinated in the sherry and cornflour mixture. As in all stir-fry recipes, it is vital that all the ingredients are assembled before cooking so that the fish and the vegetables are served the minute they are cooked.
Serves 4–6

675 g	skinned fish fillet, cod or haddock	1½ lb
30 ml	cornflour (cornstarch)	2 tbsp
	Salt and freshly ground black pepper	
30 ml	rice wine or dry sherry	2 tbsp
100 g	bamboo shoots, shredded	4 oz
100 g	Chinese leaves, cut into pieces	4 oz
	8 water chestnuts, sliced	
100 g	mangetout (snow peas)	4 oz
60 ml	oil	4 tbsp
	1 garlic clove, crushed	
150 ml	fish or chicken stock	¼ pt/⅔ cup
5 ml	sugar	1 tsp
3 cm	fresh ginger, peeled and finely shredded	1¼ in

1. Wipe the fish with kitchen paper then cut into neat-sized pieces for even cooking. Blend the cornflour, seasoning and rice wine or sherry together. Pour over the fish pieces and toss lightly.

2. Prepare all the vegetables. Heat the wok, add half the oil then gently fry the garlic without burning as this gives a bitter taste.

3. Add the vegetables and quickly stir-fry for 1 minute. Add two-thirds of the hot stock and cook rapidly for 1 more minute until the vegetables look cooked but still retain their crispness. Turn on to a plate and keep warm.

4. Heat the remaining oil in a wok, add the ginger to flavour the oil then add the fish slices and cook for 3–4 minutes until just cooked, lifting and turning gently. Add the remaining stock.

5. Return the vegetables and sauce to the pan and reheat quickly.

6. Taste for seasoning. Serve immediately on a hot serving platter with freshly cooked rice.

FISH STRIPS WITH CORN AND STRAW MUSHROOMS

CAO GU YUMI YU TIA

his recipe is a subtle blend of flavour, colour and texture which is simplicity itself. The straw mushrooms are available in cans from oriental stores as are the miniature corn. Better still, use fresh baby sweetcorn which is flown in regularly from East Africa and Thailand. They are so tender that they need only a minute or two to cook.
     Serves 3–4

450 g	fish fillet, skinned and	1 lb
	cut into neat finger-like pieces	
	Salt and freshly ground black pepper	
150 ml	chicken or fish stock	¼ pt/⅔ cup
2 cm	fresh ginger, peeled and shredded	1 in
15 ml	groundnut (peanut) oil	1 tbsp
2.5 ml	sugar	½ tsp
30 ml	rice wine or dry sherry	2 tbsp
15 ml	light soy sauce	1 tbsp
425 g	canned straw mushrooms	15 oz
100 g	baby sweetcorn	4 oz
	4 spring onions (scallions), shredded	
15 ml	sesame oil	1 tbsp

1. Place the fish pieces on a plate, season well and prepare all the other ingredients.

2. Heat the stock and ginger until boiling in a deep frying pan or wok. Carefully add the fish pieces, allow the liquid to return just to the boil.

3. Add the oil, sugar, rice wine or sherry, soy sauce, mushrooms, baby sweetcorn, most of the spring onions and seasoning to taste.

4. Bring back to the boil then reduce to a simmer. Cover with a lid and cook for about 2 minutes, depending on the size of the pieces of fish.

5. Drizzle in the sesame oil and lift out carefully on to a warmed platter. Serve garnished with the remaining spring onions.

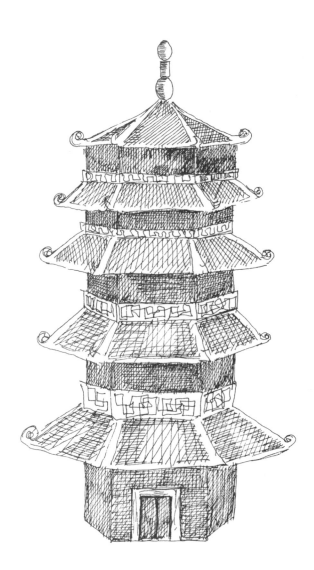

STEAMED SEA BASS
OR SEA TROUT

QING ZHENG YU

*W*hen bass or sea trout are too expensive then go for bream or a grey mullet. Again, ask the fishmonger to clean and scale the fish, leaving on the head and tail. Score the fish two or three times on each side or along the backbone to speed up the cooking as well as allowing the flavours to permeate. Bear in mind the size of the steamer you will use when buying the fish.

Serves 4 or 6 if part of a meal

	1 sea bass or trout (1 kg/2 lb) cleaned, head and tail intact	
	Salt and freshly ground black pepper	
	6 Chinese dried mushrooms, soaked in warm water for 30 minutes	
1 cm	fresh ginger, peeled and shredded	½ in
	4 spring onions (scallions), shredded	
75 ml	fish or chicken stock or soaking liquid from mushrooms	5 tbsp
30 ml	light soy sauce	2 tbsp
15 ml	sesame oil	1 tbsp

1. Wash the fish and dry well on kitchen paper. Season inside and out. Place on a large plate which will fit neatly on a rack in the wok or large shallow pan.

2. Reserve 75 ml/5 tbsp of the soaking liquid from the mushrooms if using as stock. Discard the tough stems from the mushrooms then slice the caps very finely.

3. Scatter the mushrooms, ginger and half the spring onions on top of the fish.

4. Bring a little water to the boil in the base of the steamer or wok. Place the fish in a dish on the rack to steam, covered with a tight fitting lid. If the lid is not such a good fit then cover the plate with clingfilm. Steam for about 8–12 minutes depending on the size of the fish.

5. Just before the end of the cooking, heat the stock or reserved mushroom liquid with the soy sauce, sesame oil and a little seasoning.

6. Carefully remove the plate from the steamer, pour over the hot flavoured stock and garnish with the remaining spring onions.

RED SNAPPER WITH SWEET AND SOUR SAUCE

TANG CU CHOU YU

I n one of the most popular and best loved dishes from the Cantonese cuisine, locally grown tropical fruits such as pineapple and lychees are used. Use canned when the fresh are not available. The light sauce is based on onion, garlic and ginger then thickened with cornflour. Usually shredded red pepper or chilli and spring onion will be added to make the whole dish amazingly colourful and appealing.
Serves 4–6

1 kg	1 red snapper or mullet, cleaned, head and tail intact	2 lb
Salt and freshly ground black pepper		
30 ml	cornflour (cornstarch)	2 tbsp
Oil for shallow-frying		

SAUCE:		
45 ml	tomato ketchup (catsup)	3 tbsp
15 ml	sugar	1 tbsp
30 ml	rice wine or dry sherry	2 tbsp
15 ml	light soy sauce	1 tbsp
30 ml	wine or cider vinegar	2 tbsp
10 ml	cornflour (cornstarch)	2 tsp
200 ml	fish stock or water	7 fl oz/scant 1 cup
	Salt	
30 ml	oil	2 tbsp
	1 garlic clove, crushed	
	1 small onion, sliced	
1 cm	fresh ginger, peeled and cut into shreds	½ in
	1–2 slices of pineapple, fresh or canned, cut into neat pieces	
	8 fresh or canned lychees	
	¼ green pepper, seeded and thinly sliced	
	¼ red pepper, seeded and thinly sliced	
	1 red chilli, deseeded and sliced finely	
	2 spring onions (scallions), sliced	
	Fresh coriander (cilantro) leaves	

1. Wash and dry the fish thoroughly then season and dust liberally with cornflour. Fry in shallow oil for 5–6 minutes on each side then lift out and keep warm while preparing the sauce.

2. Mix together the ketchup, sugar, rice wine or sherry, soy sauce and vinegar. Blend the cornflour with some of the measured stock or water to make a paste. Stir into the other liquids, add salt to taste and set aside.

3. Heat the oil and fry the garlic and onion without browning, stirring all the time. Add the cornflour liquid and stir until the sauce thickens.

4. Remove from the heat and add the ginger, pineapple, lychees and peppers. Taste for seasoning then pour over the cooked fish.

5. Garnish attractively with chilli, spring onions and coriander leaves.

SZECHUAN PRAWNS

GAN SHAO MING XIA

popular spicy prawn dish from Western China, the peppercorns, a reddish brown colour, are sometimes known as Chinese brown peppercorns. For best results they should be dry-fried before grinding coarsely.

Serves 4–6

675 g	fresh tiger prawns (shrimp)	1½ lb
5 ml	sugar	1 tsp
30 ml	tomato ketchup (catsup)	2 tbsp
15–30 ml	chilli sauce	1–2 tbsp
15 ml	thick soy sauce	1 tbsp
	2 garlic cloves, crushed	
1 cm	fresh ginger, peeled and finely shredded	½ in
60 ml	oil	4 tbsp
5–10 ml	Szechuan peppercorns, dry-fried and ground	1–2 tsp
15 ml	rice wine vinegar	1 tbsp
60 ml	stock or water	4 tbsp
	Salt	
	6 spring onions (scallions), finely shredded	

1. Remove the heads and body shells from the prawns but leave on the tails. Sprinkle with sugar and set aside.

2. Blend the ketchup, chilli and soy sauces together.

3. Fry the garlic and ginger in oil without browning. Add the crushed peppercorns and prawns. Toss well and when prawns are firm and pink, add the sauce mixture. Cook for 1 minute, add the vinegar, stock or water and salt to taste.

4. Now add most of the spring onions and toss well. Turn on to a serving platter garnished with remaining spring onions.

PHOENIX TAIL PRAWNS

FENG WEI XIA

he dish is so called because the tails of the prawns when cooked turn red and are reminiscent of the phoenix tail feathers. The Chinese believe that the phoenix is a sign of dignity and good luck. Fresh tiger prawns are sold head removed but with the body shell intact. These are perfect for this recipe.

Serves 6

450 g	tiger prawns (about 30) fresh or frozen and thawed	1 lb
	MARINADE:	
	1 garlic clove, crushed	
5 ml	sugar	1 tsp
15 ml	soy sauce	1 tbsp
30 ml	rice wine or dry sherry	2 tbsp
60 ml	cornflour (cornstarch)	4 tbsp
	Salt and freshly ground black pepper	
	BATTER:	
50 g	plain (all-purpose) flour	2 oz
25 g	cornflour (cornstarch)	1 oz
	1 egg, separated	
30 ml	groundnut (peanut) or sunflower oil	2 tbsp
	Oil for deep-frying	
	DIPPING:	
	Sweet and sour plum sauce, or salt and pepper mix (see page 46)	

1. Remove the claws and heads from the prawns but leave on the body shells and tails. Carefully score along the underbelly of each one and dry well on kitchen paper.

2. Blend the garlic with the sugar, soy sauce and rice wine or sherry. Pour over the prawns and set aside. Mix the 60 ml/4 tbsp of cornflour with seasoning. Leave on one side.

3. Sift the plain flour and the 25 g/1 oz of cornflour into a bowl. Just before cooking, add the strained marinade plus 45 ml/3 tbsp of water and the egg yolk and mix to a smooth batter, adding more water if necessary.

4. Stir in the oil and fold in the whisked egg white when ready to cook the prawns.

5. Heat the oil to 190°C/375°F. Dip the prawns first in the seasoned cornflour then in the prepared batter, making sure that the tails are free of batter.

6. Holding by the tails, lower into the oil. Cook about 6 at a time, allowing 2–3 minutes depending on the size of the prawns. The tails will turn red when they are cooked.

7. Lift on to kitchen paper and drain while cooking the remainder. Serve hot on a warm platter with either of the suggested accompaniments. You can buy ready-made sweet and sour plum sauce. The instructions for making salt and pepper mix are to be found on page 46, Salt and Pepper Prawns.

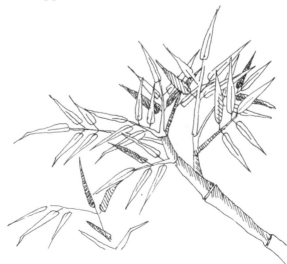

SQUID AND BLACK BEAN SAUCE

SI JIAO YOU YU

ong-winded instructions on how to clean squid used to be enough to put most people off even attempting a dish where they were the main ingredient. Now they can be bought ready cleaned on most supermarket fish counters and are inexpensive too. The first time we were served squid was in a restaurant on the shores of the South China Sea. A curious collection of what I assumed were pasta shells arrived, but in fact it was squid, cunningly scored and cut, which curl up attractively on contact with the hot wok.

Serves 4

675 g	squid, fresh or frozen and thawed	1½ lb
30–45 ml	groundnut (peanut) oil	2–3 tbsp
	2 garlic cloves, crushed	
2.5 cm	fresh ginger, peeled and shredded	1 in
	1 small onion, finely chopped	
	3 spring onions (scallions), shredded	
45 ml	salted black beans, rinsed and chopped	3 tbsp
30 ml	chilli sauce	2 tbsp
15 ml	light soy sauce	1 tbsp
	100 ml fish or chicken stock 3½ fl oz/6½ tbsp	
15 ml	cornflour (cornstarch) mixed to a thin paste with water	1 tbsp
30 ml	rice wine or dry sherry to taste	2 tbsp
	Salt and freshly ground black pepper	
15 ml	sesame oil	1 tbsp

1. Slit the cone-shaped squid from base to top lengthwise. Remove quill and discard. Rinse well. Lay flat on a board, inside uppermost, and score lightly in a lattice pattern all over the surface with the back of a knife.

2. Now cut from base to top in strips which will curl on cooking. Set aside with the tentacles which will also be cooked.

3. Prepare all the other ingredients.

4. Heat the wok without oil and toss in the well drained squid and tentacles, turning all the time until they form curls. Set aside and keep warm.

5. Rinse and dry the wok then heat the oil, add the garlic, ginger and onion, turning all the time until the onion softens.

6. Add half the spring onions and the chopped black beans, chilli and soy sauce plus the stock.

7. When bubbling, stir in the squid curls and cook for 2 minutes then thicken slightly with cornflour paste.

8. Add the seasonings of wine, salt, freshly ground black pepper and sesame oil. Serve garnished with the remaining spring onions.

KETCHUP FISH

QUIZI SHAO YU

*A pomfret is often used in this recipe, but a whole sole or plaice
are probably easier to get hold of and are equally delicious.
If you don't have a steamer large enough to hold the fish whole then it
can be cooked in a lightly greased covered dish in the oven (190°C/
375°F/gas 5) for 25 minutes.*

Serves 2, or more if part of a meal

500 g	sole or plaice, gutted, head and tail left intact	1¼ lb
	OR 2 pomfret about the same weight	
	Salt and freshly ground black pepper	
1 cm	fresh ginger, peeled and sliced into thin matchsticks	½ in
15–30 ml	groundnut (peanut) oil	1–2 tbsp

	SAUCE:	
	1 small onion, thinly sliced	
30 ml	oil	2 tbsp
15–30 ml	oyster sauce	1–2 tbsp
15–30 ml	light soy sauce	1–2 tbsp
15 ml	sesame oil	1 tbsp

	GARNISH:	
15 ml	sesame seeds, toasted	1 tbsp
	2 spring onions (scallions), shredded	

1. Wash and dry the fish. Slash two or three times on each side. Season then place in a large oiled strip of foil into an ovenproof dish which will fit into the steamer.

2. Scatter the ginger and drizzle the oil over the fish. Cover with foil. Steam for 25 minutes or bake in the oven as suggested above.

3. Fry the onion in the oil until soft and transparent then add the oyster and soy sauces. Remove from the heat.

4. When the fish is cooked, add the juices from the cooked fish to the pan. Allow to bubble, add the sesame oil and taste for seasoning.

5. Carefully transfer the fish on its foil strip to a warmed serving dish and pour over the hot sauce. Garnish with sesame seeds and scatter with spring onions.

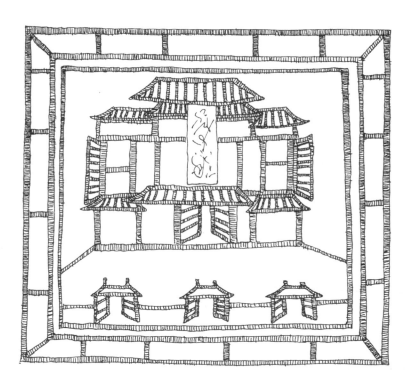

KUNG PAO PRAWN

KUNG PO XIA

his dish is supposedly named after Kung Pao, a bureaucrat who was discreetly posted from Peking to Szechuan. In the Kung Pao style of cooking, the main ingredient is quickly fried until crisp but tender and is added at the last minute to a sauce which is a clever balance of hot, sweet and sour flavours in the true Szechuan style.
      Serves 4

450 g	large prawns (shrimp), thawed if frozen	1 lb
30 ml	cornflour (cornstarch)	2 tbsp
	Salt and freshly ground black pepper	
	3 spring onions (scallions)	
300 ml	groundnut (peanut) or sunflower oil for frying	½ pt/1¼ cups
	3 garlic cloves, crushed	
1 cm	ginger, peeled and cut into thin strips	½ in
60 ml	rice wine vinegar	4 tbsp
30 ml	light brown sugar	2 tbsp
30 ml	light soy sauce	2 tbsp
5 ml	Szechuan peppercorns, dry-fried and crushed	1 tsp

1. Dry the prawns thoroughly on kitchen paper. Season the cornflour on a piece of greaseproof paper on a plate. Pour the oil into a wok. Prepare the remaining ingredients. Chop the white part of the spring onions for the sauce and shred the top for garnish.

2. When ready to cook, heat the oil to 190°C/375°F. Toss the prawns in the cornflour then fry in hot oil, turning all the time until crisp. This will take only 2 minutes depending on the size of the prawns.

3. Drain on kitchen paper and keep warm. Pour off all except 30 ml/2 tbsp of oil from the wok and use the remainder when cooking fish on another occasion.

4. Heat this 30 ml/2 tbsp of oil and fry the garlic, ginger and white part of spring onions quickly without browning. Add the vinegar, sugar, soy sauce and Szechuan peppercorns. Allow to come back to the boil.

5. Add the prawns and cook for 30 seconds. Taste for seasoning. Serve at once garnished with shredded spring onion tops.

STEAMED SCALLOPS WITH BLACK BEAN SAUCE

SI ZI ZHENG ZIAN BI

This recipe is one which I have adapted from the dish I enjoyed in the Oriental Restaurant at the Dorchester. Spoil yourself and buy the large scallops rather than the Queen size for a more handsome-looking presentation.

Serves 3–4 as part of a meal

450 g	large scallops, rinsed and dried	1 lb
15 ml	salted black beans	1 tbsp
	Pinch of salt	
5 ml	sugar	1 tsp
5 ml	dark soy sauce	1 tsp
2.5 ml	sesame oil	½ tsp
15 ml	rice wine or dry sherry	1 tbsp
15 ml	oyster sauce	1 tbsp
10 ml	cornflour (cornstarch)	2 tsp
	1 garlic clove, crushed	
	2 spring onions (scallions), shredded	
	1 stem coriander (cilantro), leaves removed for garnish	
30 ml	corn or sunflower oil	2 tbsp

1. Remove the corals carefully from the scallops. Slice the white fleshy part through horizontally to make 2 rounds. Arrange the scallop rounds and corals neatly in a shallow ovenproof dish which will fit into the steamer or on to a trivet in the wok. I used a quiche dish (23 cm/9 in) which was ideal.

2. Make up the sauce by lightly crushing the black beans with the back of a spoon in a bowl. Add the salt, sugar, soy sauce, sesame oil, rice wine or sherry, oyster sauce and cornflour and mix well. Make a broad ribbon of foil and place under the cooking dish to ease lifting in and out of the steamer.

3. Assemble the garlic, spring onions and coriander leaves. Place the oil into a small pan ready to heat when required.

4. About 10 minutes before serving, pour the sauce over the scallops, cover with clingfilm and place in a large steamer with plenty of fast boiling water then cover with a tight fitting lid and steam for 10 minutes.

5. Test the scallops with a skewer; they will be meltingly tender. Scatter with the garlic, spring onion and coriander.

6. Heat the oil and pour over the top just before taking to the table. This brings out the complementary flavours of all the ingredients beautifully.

7. Serve at once with freshly cooked rice straight from the cooking dish set on a large cold plate so that guests and host will not burn their hands!

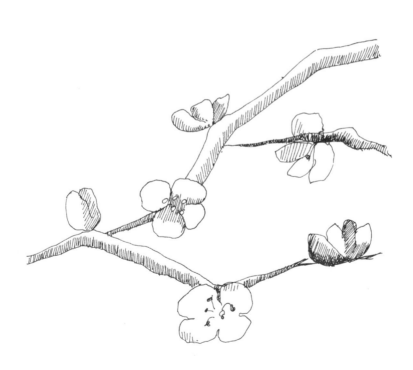

DUCK

STIR-FRY ROAST DUCK WITH BEAN SPROUTS

DAO YA CHAO YA

real quickie recipe, this can be easily assembled and cooked in a twinkling. A marvellous way to use up some leftover duckling from the family roast.

Serves 2–3

225–300 g	cooked duckling meat, cut into neat slices	8–12 oz
Juices from cooking of duckling if available		
15 ml	oyster sauce	1 tbsp
15 ml	rice wine or sherry	1 tbsp
30 ml	water	2 tbsp
200 g	bean sprouts	7 oz
4–6 spring onions (scallions), chopped		
30–45 ml	groundnut (peanut) oil	2–3 tbsp
Salt and freshly ground black pepper		

1. Set the duck meat aside. Melt the pan juices from the cooked duckling and blend with oyster sauce, rice wine or sherry and water.

2. Blanch the bean sprouts by plunging into boiling water and drain immediately, or pour some boiling water over the bean sprouts in a colander or sieve. Rinse with cold water to halt the cooking.

3. Fry most of the spring onions in hot oil until the onion has wilted. Add the duck meat and stir-fry over high heat followed by bean sprouts and the sauce mixture. Taste for seasoning.

4. Serve garnished with the remaining spring onions.

EMPEROR'S PEKING DUCK

BEIJING KAO JA

his dish is a lot of fun – which may well account for the fact that Peking duck is undoubtedly the best loved duck recipe featured on every Chinese restaurant menu. Taste it and you'll know why. That said, it takes time to prepare, but like bread making which has the same image, start preparation the day before, then cook and serve the next evening.

Home-made Mandarin pancakes, to be served with this dish, may make you feel a virtuous hostess but you can also buy them from your local Chinese takeaway, oriental supermarket or large supermarket chain. Use the duckling bones for a delicious soup.

Serves 4–6 as a main course and more as a starter

2.25 kg	duckling, fresh or frozen and thawed	about 5 lb
	Salt	
45 ml	honey	3 tbsp
10 ml	hot water	2 tsp
15 ml	light soy sauce	1 tbsp

TO SERVE:
Mandarin Pancakes (see page 112)
1 bunch spring onions (scallions)
½–1 cucumber
Hoisin and plum sauces

1. Rinse the duck then either plunge it into a large pan of boiling water or pour a kettle full of boiling water over the duck in the sink. This scalds and firms up the skin. Remove any quills from the bird. Sprinkle the inside with salt.

2. Secure the legs with string and leave to drip over a bowl in a cool airy place overnight.

3. Next day, blend the honey, water and soy sauce together and brush the skin of the suspended duck with this mixture three times, allowing it to dry between each brushing. This gives the famous lacquered look.

4. Set the duckling on a rack over a roasting tin and place in the centre of a very hot oven at 230°C/450°F/gas 8 then immediately reduce the oven temperature to 180°C/350°F/gas 4 and cook for 1½ hours. Do not baste.

5. Check that the skin is crispy about 15 minutes before the end of cooking and if necessary raise the oven temperature.

6. Meanwhile prepare the pancakes. Trim the root from the spring onions. Cut into 5 cm/2 in lengths and shred finely. Cut the cucumber into thick matchstick-like pieces. Arrange on a serving platter and spoon the sauces into dishes.

7. Carve the duckling at the table, removing the skin in neat pieces. The meat can be carved separately, but to be authentic should be shredded using two forks.

8. Each guest then spreads a little of the sauce on to a pancake, tops with a modest amount of crisp skin, the shredded meat, cucumber and spring onion, rolls up the pancake and savours each mouthful.

AROMATIC CRISPY DUCK

XIANG SU YA

nother classic recipe, this duckling is served in a similar way to the Peking duck but is first marinated in spices then steamed until tender and finally deep-fried to give it its characteristic crispness. In some recipes the duckling might first be braised in a rich stock then allowed to dry before deep-frying. For home cooking I recommend cutting the duck into at least half or even quarters to make it more manageable. You can buy quarter portions of duckling from most large supermarkets.

Serves 4–5

1 duckling (2.25 kg/about 5 lb) or portions		
10 ml	salt	2 tsp
2.5 ml	black pepper or Szechuan peppercorns, dry-fried and crushed	½ tsp
5 ml	five-spice powder	1 tsp
45 ml	light soy sauce	3 tbsp
45 ml	rice wine or dry sherry	3 tbsp
10 ml	clear honey	2 tsp
1 cm	fresh ginger, peeled and grated	½ in
1 bunch spring onions (scallions), chopped		
Oil for deep-frying		

TO SERVE:
Mandarin Pancakes (page 112) or Steamed Flower Rolls (page 60)
1 bunch spring onions (scallions), finely shredded
½ cucumber, cut into matchsticks
Hoisin and/or plum sauce

1. Divide the duckling in half, wipe with kitchen paper and prick the skin lightly with a fork. Do the same if using portions. Rub all over the skin with salt.

2. Blend together the black pepper or ground peppercorns, five-spice powder, soy sauce, rice wine or sherry, honey and ginger. Rub all over the duckling and leave to marinate for 3–4 hours, basting from time to time.

3. Place the duckling pieces into a steamer set on a bed of chopped spring onions and steam gently for 2 hours or until tender.

4. Alternatively, set the duck on a bed of spring onions on a plate. Place this on a trivet in a deep roasting tin which is half full with boiling water. Cover with a foil lid. Cook in a hot oven at 220°C/425°F/gas 7 for 1 hour then reduce the heat to 190°C/375°F/gas 5 for 1 hour or until the duckling is tender. Top up with water as necessary. Handle with great care and a steady hand.

5. Drain the duckling on a trivet. Reserve the cooking juices to add to the bones when making stock. Leave the duckling to dry for 4–6 hours.

6. Just before serving, prepare the accompaniments and heat the oil. Deep-fry the duckling portions for 2–3 minutes then remove from the pan, reheat the oil and deep-fry again for a further 2–3 minutes to ensure that the skin is really crisp.

7. Remove the duckling meat and skin from the bones, cut into small pieces and serve in Mandarin Pancakes (page 112) as for Peking duck. Alternatively place the meat and sauces in a lettuce leaf, roll up into a parcel and eat with Steamed Flower Rolls (page 60).

TEA-SMOKED ROAST DUCKLING

ZHAGCHA YAZI

*L*apsang Souchong with its smoky, tarry flavour is perhaps the best tea leaf to choose for your first attempt at this unusual recipe. The duckling is first smoked and then roasted. Again it is served with Mandarin Pancakes, spring onion, cucumber and sauces and then wrapped up into a delicious mouthful as for Peking duck. You might like to try cooking a chicken in the same way. As an alternative serving suggestion for either duckling or chicken, allow to go cold after roasting then serve slices with a few attractive salad leaves as a starter. Use a heavy-weight wok or metal casserole for this recipe. Choose a day when all the windows can be opened as even though the smoke should be sealed in the tightly covered wok, smells do pervade the kitchen.

Serves 4–6

	1 duckling (2.25 kg/about 5 lb)	
50 g	tea leaves, Lapsang Souchong or Keemun	2 oz
50 g	golden granulated sugar	2 oz
100 g	plain (all-purpose) flour	4 oz
10 ml	Szechuan peppercorns, dry-fried	2 tsp
2.5 cm	fresh ginger, peeled and sliced	1 in
30 ml	rice wine or dry sherry	2 tbsp
	6 spring onions (scallions), chopped	

TO SERVE:
Mandarin Pancakes (see page 112)
1 bunch spring onions (scallions), finely shredded
½–1 cucumber, cut into matchsticks
Hoisin and plum sauces

1. Dry the duckling thoroughly and prick the skin lightly.

2. Line the wok with kitchen foil. Mix the tea leaves, sugar and flour together and spoon on to the foil. Place the duckling on a trivet and carefully set into the wok. Cover with a well-fitting lid or make a lid of foil.

3. Set over a high heat. Soon the tea mixture will smoke fiercely. Reduce the heat but make sure that there is still plenty of smoke for 30 minutes. The duck skin will turn a rich mahogany colour.

4. Meanwhile, crush the peppercorns, add the ginger and pound well. Moisten this mixture with the rice wine or sherry.

5. Lift the duckling on the trivet from the wok and place in a roasting tin. Brush with the crushed ingredients, add the spring onions to the remainder and spoon into the body cavity.

6. Set to roast in a hot oven at 200°C/400°F/gas 6 for 1¼–1½ hours until the skin is crisp.

7. Serve cut into slices with accompaniments as for Peking duck.

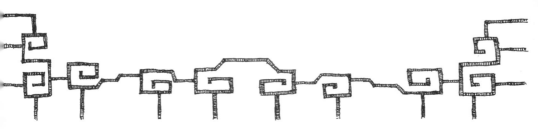

KAIFENG SOY DUCK

JIANG YA

*W*e enjoyed this wonderful duckling dish at the Kaifeng, which is a popular Kosher Chinese restaurant in north London. A duckling is braised in a rich well seasoned and spiced soy-based stock until really tender, by which time it will have taken on a glorious mahogany colour. Traditionally the duckling is chopped into small pieces before serving so that it can be eaten with chopsticks.

Serves 4, or more as part of a buffet

	1 duckling (2.25 kg/about 5 lb)	
150 ml	dark soy sauce	¼ pt/⅔ cup
150 ml	light soy sauce	¼ pt/⅔ cup
300 ml	warm water	½ pt/1¼ cups
50 g	coffee sugar crystals or dark brown sugar	2 oz/¼ cup
5 ml	coriander (cilantro) seed	1 tsp
5 ml	cumin seed	1 tsp
5 ml	fennel seed	1 tsp
	6 cardamom pods	
	6 cloves	
	2 star anise	
	1 cinnamon stick	
	1 strip dried tangerine peel or fresh orange peel without pith	
2 cm	fresh ginger, peeled and shredded	1 in
	1 bunch spring onions (scallions), chopped	
15-30 ml	arrowroot blended to a paste with water	1-2 tbsp
	Fresh coriander (cilantro) leaves	
	1 red chilli, shredded	

1. Rinse the duckling and set aside. Pour the soy sauces and water into a flameproof casserole sufficiently large enough to hold the duckling comfortably. Add the sugar and allow to simmer gently, stirring until the sugar dissolves.

2. Meanwhile place all the spices into a square of muslin (cheesecloth) (pound together first if you like) and tie up into a bouquet garni and place into the casserole.

3. Place the ginger and chopped spring onions into the body cavity of the duckling then place in the casserole breast-side down for the first hour, simmering gently.

4. Turn the duckling over on to its back and cook a further hour.

5. Turn the duckling breast-side down and allow to cool in the liquid for at least 30 minutes.

6. Lift the duckling out of the casserole and divide the two leg portions into half. The breasts can be neatly sliced. Arrange the duckling on a platter.

7. Discard the bag of spices then skin the fat from the stock. Reheat the cooking liquid and thicken with the arrowroot to a rich glossy sauce. Spoon over the duckling portions and serve hot or warm, with the coriander leaves and shredded chilli scattered on top.

STEAMED DUCK BREASTS WITH PINEAPPLE AND PRESERVED GINGER

ZILO YA SI

U se the boneless duckling breasts which are widely available for this recipe. Alternatively use the whole bird which would be much more economical as the legs can be used for another meal and the carcass for a tasty soup. Much more in line with Chinese thinking! Serves 2–3 if using breasts only

	2 boneless duckling breast fillets or 1 whole duckling (2 kg/4 lb)	
	Salt and freshly ground black pepper	
	4 spring onions (scallions), chopped	
15 ml	light soy sauce	1 tbsp
225 g	canned pineapple rings and 90 ml/6 tbsp juice	8 oz
	4 pieces Chinese stem ginger in syrup	
45 ml	ginger syrup	3 tbsp
	Pinch of salt	
	¼ red (bell) pepper, deseeded and cut in thin strips	
	¼ green (bell) pepper, deseeded and cut in thin strips	
30 ml	cornflour (cornstarch) mixed to a paste with water	2 tbsp

1. Place the breasts in a bowl, sprinkle with salt and pepper and set on a bed of chopped spring onions. Cover with clingfilm.

2. Set in a steamer and steam the breasts for 1 hour until tender.

3. When slightly cooled, slice the breasts into thin slices and lay on a platter moistened with a little of the cooking juices from the steaming bowl. Cover and keep warm whilst preparing the sauce.

4. Pour the pineapple juice into a pan with an equal amount of water and the strained cooking juices from cooking the duck breasts. Add the syrup from the ginger and a pinch of salt then heat gently.

5. Cut the pineapple and ginger into attractive slices and arrange on top of the duck slices with the pepper strips.

6. Stir the cornflour into the juices in the pan to thicken. Pour over the duck and serve at once.

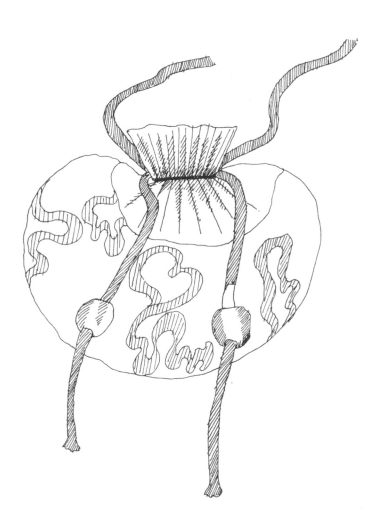

SAUTÉED FILLET OF DUCK WITH BLACK BEAN SAUCE

SI ZHI YA PIAN

popular recipe from the Oriental Restaurant at the Dorchester which proudly boasts the award of a Michelin star.
Serves 4

2 duckling breasts, about 375 g/13 oz		
5 ml	sugar	1 tsp
15 ml	rice wine or dry sherry	2 tbsp
2.5 ml	cornflour (cornstarch) mixed with 5 ml/1 tsp water	½ tsp
Salt and freshly ground black pepper		
1 green (bell) pepper, deseeded and diced		
1 red chilli, deseeded and sliced		
1 garlic clove, crushed		
100 g	canned straw mushrooms	4 oz
15 ml	black beans, rinsed and pounded	1 tbsp

	SAUCE:	
5 ml	rice wine or dry sherry	1 tsp
45 ml	chicken stock or water	3 tbsp
5 ml	oyster sauce	1 tsp
5 ml	dark soy sauce	1 tsp
5 ml	sesame oil	1 tsp
5 ml	sugar	1 tsp

45 ml	oil	3 tbsp
2.5 ml	cornflour (cornstarch) mixed with 5 ml/1 tsp water	½ tsp

1. Slice the duck breasts thinly across the grain and then mix with the sugar, rice wine or sherry, cornflour and seasoning to taste.

2. Prepare the pepper, chilli, garlic, straw mushrooms and black beans.

3. Mix together the remaining ingredients except for the oil and cornflour paste for thickening the sauce.

4. Heat the wok, add half the oil and stir-fry the duckling for 3–4 minutes until tender, stirring all the time.

5. Lift out and keep warm. Heat the remaining oil and fry the vegetables for 1 minute then pour in the flavouring sauces.

6. Return the duckling to the pan and thicken with the remaining cornflour paste. Serve at once.

STIR-FRY ROAST DUCK WITH LYCHEES

LYCHEE CHAO YA

A typical Cantonese recipe, this makes full use of the wonderful tropical fruit which grows so profusely in Southern China. Serves 2–3

	½ Roast Honey Duck (see page 117), allowed to go cold	
550 g	canned lychees	1¼ lb
2.5 cm	fresh ginger, peeled and cut into fine shreds	1 in
45 ml	groundnut (peanut) or sunflower oil	3 tbsp
175 g	mangetout	6 oz
5 ml	cornflour (cornstarch) mixed into a paste with a little juice from the lychees	1 tsp
	Salt and freshly ground black pepper	
	Fresh coriander (cilantro) leaves	

1. Trim the meat from the bones of the duck into neat even-sized pieces. Use the bones to make stock or soup.

2. Drain the juice from the lychees and reserve.

3. When ready to serve, stir-fry the ginger shreds in 30 ml/ 2 tbsp of the oil till softened. Add the mangetout and fry quickly till they take on a rich green colour. Remove from the wok at once.

4. Add the remaining oil to the wok then add the roast duck slices, tossing for 1 minute. Add 150 ml/¼ pt/⅔ cup of the reserved lychee juice and bring to the boil. Thicken with cornflour paste.

5. Reduce the heat, add the lychees and mangetout and taste for seasoning. Serve garnished with coriander leaves.

ROAST HONEY DUCK

SHAO YA

*D*elicious eaten either hot or cold, the meat can also be cut into
   neat slices to use in almost any stir-fry recipe.
Serves 4

	1 duck (2 kg/4 lb)	
30 ml	rice wine or orange juice	2 tbsp
30 ml	light soy sauce	2 tbsp
15 ml	dark brown sugar	1 tbsp
30 ml	clear honey	2 tbsp
5 ml	salt	1 tsp

1. Rinse the duckling and dry with kitchen paper. Prick the skin lightly with a fork.

2. Blend the rest of the ingredients in a glass or stainless steel bowl and place the duckling breast-side down in this mixture to marinate for at least an hour, basting from time to time.

3. Place the duckling on a trivet over a roasting tin. Pour in water to a depth of 2.5 cm/1 in. Roast the duckling in a moderately hot oven at 190°C/375°F/gas 5 for 2 hours, basting from time to time with the reserved marinade. Cover loosely with foil to prevent overbrowning if necessary.

4. Serve cut into small pieces suitable for eating with chopsticks.

MANDARIN PANCAKES

BAO BING

225 g	strong white plain8 oz/1/2 cups (all-purpose) flour	
1.5 ml	salt	¼ tsp
200 ml	boiling water	7 fl oz/scant 1 cup
45 ml	groundnut (peanut) or sesame oil 3 tbsp	

1. Sift the flour and salt together into a bowl or food processor.

2. Gradually add sufficient water and 15 ml/1 tbsp of the oil to make a soft but not sticky dough.

3. Knead for 2–3 minutes on a lightly floured board or for 30 seconds in a processor.

4. Cover and allow to rest for 30 minutes then divide the dough into 20 pieces.

5. Roll out each piece of dough into 13–15 cm/5–6 in rounds. Brush the surface of half the rounds with oil and sandwich in pairs. Cook immediately by using two frying pans to speed up the process.

6. Lightly brush the surface of each pan with oil and cook the pancakes, still sandwiched together, on each side till puffy but not brown. This will take 3–4 minutes in all.

7. Pull the pancakes apart and pile up on a plate with a round of baking parchment between each. Cover with a lid of foil while cooking the remainder.

8. Serve hot or set aside covered with foil until required then reheat on the same plate in a steamer or in a microwave (remove the foil if using the microwave).

9. Any leftover pancakes can be frozen and reheated by either steaming in a covered container for 10 minutes or putting in a microwave for 20–30 seconds.

CHICKEN

PAPER-WRAPPED CHICKEN

ZHI BAO JI

*I*n China, little parcels of marinated chicken or fish would be wrapped in cellophane paper and then deep-fried. It is a style of cooking peculiar to Chinese cuisine and a perfect way of keeping all the flavours and aromas together which are revealed when each diner opens their parcel. The parcels take only a few minutes to cook. Drain well on absorbent paper and serve immediately.

Makes about 12 parcels

2 boneless chicken breasts (300 g/11 oz), skin removed		
45 ml	light soy sauce	3 tbsp
15 ml	rice wine or dry sherry	1 tbsp
5-10 ml	sugar	1-2 tsp
Freshly ground black pepper		
2 cm	fresh ginger, peeled and grated	¾ in
1 bunch spring onions (scallions)		
100 g	cooked ham	4 oz
Oil for deep-frying		
Stir-fry mangetout or broccoli to serve		

1. Cut the chicken into small finger-sized pieces.

2. Marinate in a mixture of soy sauce, rice wine or sherry, sugar, black pepper and ginger.

3. Cut the spring onions into 5 cm/2 in strips and the ham into finger-sized pieces.

4. Prepare 18 cm/7 in squares of cellophane or greaseproof paper to make the wrappers.

5. Brush the paper with oil then lay a piece of chicken and marinade in the centre and top with spring onion. Top with ham and a second piece of chicken.

6. Fold the paper almost corner to corner to make a triangle.

7. Fold the sides to the middle to make an envelope shape then tuck in the flap to make a neat parcel.

8. Secure with a paper clip if necessary but remember to warn your guests when they open their parcels. Repeat with the remaining ingredients.

9. Heat the oil to 190°C/375°F and fry several parcels at a time for 2-3 minutes. Do not overcook or allow the paper to turn brown.

10. Drain thoroughly and serve hot garnished with mangetout or broccoli.

BANG BANG CHICKEN

BON BON JI

hat a wonderful and quite unforgettable name for this special dish from Szechuan! Use sesame seed paste (tahini) for the authentic flavoured sauce. However, crunchy peanut butter can be used equally well; it gives extra texture to the sauce which is simply poured on top of the thin slivers of cooked chicken. A good dish to serve for a crowd as it can be made in advance.

Serves 4

3 boneless chicken breasts, about 450 g/1 lb		
1 small onion, halved		
1 garlic clove, crushed		
Salt and freshly ground black pepper		

	SAUCE:	
45 ml	tahini, and	3 tbsp
45 ml	chicken stock	3 tbsp
	OR	
45 ml	crunchy peanut butter and	3 tbsp
30 ml	sesame oil	2 tbsp
15 ml	light soy sauce	1 tbsp
15 ml	wine vinegar	1 tbsp
2 spring onions (scallions), finely chopped		
2 garlic cloves, crushed		
1 cm	fresh ginger, peeled and grated	½ in
15 ml	Szechuan peppercorns, dry-fried and crushed	1 tbsp
5 ml	light brown sugar	1 tsp

	CHILLI OIL:	
60 ml	groundnut (peanut) oil	4 tbsp
5 ml	chilli powder	1 tsp

TO SERVE:

1 cucumber, peeled, deseeded and cut into
matchstick-like pieces

1. Place the chicken in a saucepan. Just cover with water, add the onion and garlic, bring to the boil, skim then add the seasoning. Cover and cook for 25 minutes until just tender.

2. Prepare the sauce by blending the tahini with some of the stock from cooking the chicken or the peanut butter with the sesame oil.

3. Add the soy sauce, vinegar, spring onions, garlic, ginger, crushed peppercorns and sugar to taste.

4. Prepare the chilli oil by gently heating the oil and chilli powder together until foaming. Simmer for 2 minutes, remove from the heat and cool then strain off the red coloured oil and discard the sediment.

5. Make a bed of sliced cucumber, cut into chunky matchstick-like pieces and top with the chicken sliced in the same way. Top with the sauce and then drizzle on the chilli oil.

6. Guests toss their own helping on their plate before eating.

SZECHUAN-STYLE CHICKEN WITH TANGERINE PEEL AND SPICES

CHEN PI JI

This recipe fully encapsulates the flavours of Szechuan cooking with all the taste sensations of hot, sour, sweet and salty blended together.

Serves 6, or more as part of a buffet

	1 chicken, about 1.5 kg/3½ lb	
45 ml	light soy sauce	3 tbsp
15 ml	dark soy sauce	1 tbsp
45 ml	rice wine or dry sherry	3 tbsp
	4 spring onions (scallions), chopped	
	1–2 dried chillis, dry-fried and crushed	
5 ml	Szechuan peppercorns, dry-fried and crushed	1 tsp
	1 long piece of tangerine peel, crushed (see page 38)	
50 g	cornflour (cornstarch) seasoned with salt and pepper	2 oz/½ cup
	Oil for deep-frying	
30 ml	rice wine vinegar	2 tbsp
20 ml	dark brown sugar	4 tsp
150 ml	chicken stock	¼ pt/⅔ cup

1. Wipe the chicken, cut into quarters and then cut each piece into three. You will now have twelve pieces, which can be picked up and eaten with chopsticks by the proficient or with the fingers if you prefer!

2. Mix the soy sauces, rice wine or sherry, and two of the spring onions in a glass or plastic bowl. Marinate the chicken pieces in this for 3–4 hours.

3. Prepare the remaining ingredients. Leave the seeds in the dried chilli only if you like the dish to be hot.

4. About 45 minutes before serving, place the chicken pieces on a trivet over a large tray to collect the marinade. Reserve to use later.

5. Dust the chicken pieces with seasoned cornflour and deep-fry in two or three batches in hot oil at 190°C/375°F for about 8–10 minutes until crisp and brown and cooked through. Keep warm.

6. Spoon 45 ml/3 tbsp of the oil into a pan and fry the crushed chillies, peppercorns and tangerine for 30 seconds.

7. Add the cooked chicken pieces, stir over a medium to high heat then add the vinegar and cook until the vinegar evaporates.

8. Add the sugar, marinade and stock then cook together without covering, stirring from time to time until the liquid almost evaporates and all the flavours are captured in the chicken pieces.

9. Serve at once garnished with the reserved spring onions.

SWEET AND SOUR CHICKEN

TANG CU JI

*P*erhaps the most popular sauce in the Chinese restaurant repertoire, this sauce, of Cantonese origin, should be quite light in texture with delectable sweet and sour flavours and jewel-coloured pieces of crunchy vegetable.

Serves 4, or more as part of a buffet

3 boneless chicken breasts, about 450 g/1 lb		
75 ml	oil for frying	5 tbsp
	SAUCE:	
3 canned pineapple rings plus 150 ml/¼ pt/⅔ cup juice		
1 carrot, cut into flowers (see p. 169)		
½ red (bell) pepper, deseeded and thinly sliced		
½ green (bell) pepper, deseeded and thinly sliced		
8 canned water chestnuts, sliced		
1 small onion, thinly sliced		
1 garlic clove, crushed		
10 ml	tomato purée (paste)	2 tsp
60 ml	wine vinegar	4 tbsp
15–30 ml	brown sugar	1–2 tbsp
120 ml	water	4 fl oz/½ cup
10 ml	light soy sauce	2 tsp
10 ml	cornflour (cornstarch) blended to a paste with 30 ml/2 tbsp water	2 tsp
Salt and freshly ground black pepper		
Fresh coriander (cilantro) leaves or shredded spring onion to garnish		

1. Remove the skin from the chicken and cut into even-sized pieces.

2. Prepare all the other ingredients. Place small pieces of pineapple, carrot flowers, peppers and water chestnuts in piles on a tray with the onion and garlic.

3. Blend the tomato purée, vinegar, sugar, water and soy sauce in a bowl. In a separate bowl, blend the cornflour with the 30 ml/2 tbsp of water and the pineapple juice.

4. When ready to cook, heat the wok then add half the oil and fry the chicken pieces, turning frequently, for 7–8 minutes until cooked through. Keep warm.

5. Add the remaining oil to the wok, fry the onion and crushed garlic for 1 minute without browning then add the vinegar and sugar mixture and bring to the boil.

6. Add the reserved pineapple juice and blended cornflour, return to the heat and stir until the sauce thickens slightly.

7. Add the pineapple pieces, carrot, peppers and water chestnuts. Allow to return just to the boil then add the cooked chicken pieces and cook briefly in the sauce. Taste and adjust the seasoning to taste.

8. Serve immediately garnished with coriander leaves or shredded spring onion.

CHICKEN WITH CASHEW NUTS

YAO GUA CHAO JIN DING

A delightful blend of textures, flavours and colours to tempt any of your guests. Use walnuts or almonds if cashew nuts are not available.

Serves 2, or more as part of a meal

	2 chicken breasts, about 275 g/10 oz	
	1 egg white	
30 ml	rice wine or dry sherry	2 tbsp
10 ml	cornflour (cornstarch)	2 tsp
	Salt and freshly ground black pepper	
90 ml	oil for frying	6 tbsp
100 g	cashew nuts, walnuts or almonds	4 oz/1 cup
	2 spring onions (scallions), chopped	
100 g	button mushrooms, thinly sliced	4 oz
100 g	mangetout	4 oz
15 ml	light soy sauce	1 tbsp
60 ml	chicken stock or water	4 tbsp
5 ml	cornflour (cornstarch) blended to a paste with water	1 tsp
	Fresh coriander (cilantro) leaves to garnish	

1. Trim the skin from the chicken and cut into fine shreds. Allow to cook over a gentle heat in the wok until crisp and golden with the chicken oil left in the base of the wok. Drain the chicken skin on kitchen paper for use as a garnish. The chicken oil can be used later in the recipe.

2. Cut the chicken into thin even-sized pieces. Lightly whisk the egg white to a froth then add the wine or sherry, cornflour and seasoning. Toss the chicken pieces in this mixture.

3. Heat the oil from rendering the skin with 30 ml/2 tbsp of the oil and fry the chicken pieces until golden, turning all the time. Set aside and keep warm.

4. Spoon a further 30 ml/2 tbsp of oil into another pan and fry the cashew nuts, walnuts or almonds until golden. Reserve.

5. Heat the remaining oil in a clean pan and fry the spring onion, mushroom slices and mangetout for 1-2 minutes until the mangetout are a rich green colour.

6. Add the soy sauce and stock then add the cornflour paste and stir until the sauce thickens slightly.

7. Add the chicken and stir over a high heat for 30 seconds. Finally add most of the nuts. Serve garnished with the remainder of the nuts, crisp pieces of chicken skin and coriander.

DICED CHICKEN WITH PEPPERS AND YELLOW BEAN SAUCE

CHING CHIAO JI DING

oneless chicken breasts are a godsend in a recipe such as this. However, I rather suspect that the shrewd Chinese would always buy the whole bird in order to make at least two more dishes from it, underlining the age old conflict of time versus expediency!
Serves 2–3

2 boneless chicken breasts, about 375 g/13 oz		
6 Chinese dried mushrooms, soaked in warm water for 30 minutes		
30 ml	yellow bean sauce	2 tbsp
45 ml	rice wine or sherry	3 tbsp
15 ml	light soy sauce	1 tbsp
5 ml	dark brown sugar	1 tsp
½ red (bell) pepper, deseeded and cubed		
½ green (bell) pepper, deseeded and cubed		
1 garlic clove, crushed		
1 cm	fresh ginger, peeled and shredded	½ in
45 ml	groundnut (peanut) oil	3 tbsp
5 ml	cornflour (cornstarch) blended to a paste with water	1 tsp

1. Skin the chicken and cut into even-sized cubes.

2. Discard the stems from the mushrooms and slice the caps thinly. Add 75 ml/5 tbsp of soaking water from the mushrooms to the bean sauce with the rice wine or sherry, soy sauce and brown sugar and reserve.

3. Prepare the other ingredients and set on a tray ready for cooking.

4. Heat the oil and quickly fry the garlic and ginger. Do not allow to brown but just give off a beautiful aroma.

5. Add the chicken cubes and quickly stir-fry for 2 minutes then add the mushroom slices with the peppers.

6. When the peppers look glossy, add the sauce mixture and cook rapidly for a further 2 minutes, adding a little more of the mushroom water if necessary.

7. At the last minute, stir in the cornflour paste to thicken and serve at once on a hot plate.

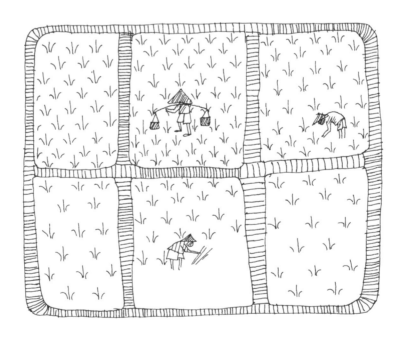

GINGER CHICKEN

CONG YOU JI

*I*n spite of the rather generous amount of ginger, it merely complements the other flavours rather than dominating. I like to slice the peeled ginger very thinly then shred it into fine matchstick-like pieces.

Serves 4–5

4 boneless chicken breasts, about 675 g/1½ lb		
5 ml	sugar	1 tsp
Salt and freshly ground black pepper		
9–10 cm piece of fresh ginger, peeled, thinly sliced and cut into matchsticks		3½–4 in
60 ml	sunflower oil	4 tbsp
100 g	button mushrooms or canned straw mushrooms	4 oz
100 ml	chicken stock or water	3½ fl oz/ 6½ tbsp
30 ml	brandy	2 tbsp
10 ml	cornflour (cornstarch) blended to a paste with 45ml/3 tbsp cold water	2 tsp
5 ml	soy sauce	1 tsp
Fresh coriander (cilantro) leaves to garnish		

1. Skin the chicken breasts and cut into thin slivers. Sprinkle with sugar and leave to stand for at least 15 minutes. Season.

2. Fry the ginger in hot oil without browning, then add the chicken and cook, stirring all the time, for 2–3 minutes.

3. Add the mushrooms and cook for 1 minute then add the stock or water and bring to the boil. Reduce the heat and cover with a lid. Cook for 4 minutes, when the chicken pieces will be tender.

4. Add the brandy, cornflour paste and soy sauce and stir until the sauce thickens. Taste and adjust the seasoning. Serve garnished with coriander leaves.

CANTONESE LEMON CHICKEN

NING MENG JI

here are two different cooking styles for this recipe, either steamed or deep-fried. I have selected the recipe where the chicken is steamed, which allows the lemon flavour to permeate the velvety, tender chicken meat. Served cold it is the ideal starter for a meal or a perfect luncheon dish with its clean flavours and pretty pale colours.

Serves 4, or more as part of a meal

1.25 kg	fresh chicken or 2 poussin	3 lb
	2 large lemons	
	Salt and freshly ground black pepper	
	6 Chinese dried mushrooms, soaked in warm water for 30 minutes	
4 cm	fresh ginger, peeled and shredded	1½ in
15 ml	groundnut (peanut) or sunflower oil	1 tbsp
30 ml	sugar to taste	2 tbsp

GARNISH:
Fresh coriander (cilantro) leaves
½ green or red (bell) pepper, deseeded and shredded

1. Rinse and dry the chicken. Place in an ovenproof dish which will fit in a large flameproof casserole or on a trivet in the wok.

2. Using a potato peeler, pare the rind from one of the lemons and cut into fine shreds. Finely grate the rind of the second lemon, squeeze the juice from both and reserve.

3. Place the squeezed lemon shells round the chicken and season the skin with salt and pepper. Steam for about 1¼–1½ hours or until quite tender.

4. In the meantime, drain the mushrooms, discard the stems and slice the caps thinly. Prepare the ginger.

5. When the chicken is cooked, allow to cool then remove the skin. Cut the breasts from the bone and slice into three pieces. Remove the legs and cut each into two portions. Reserve the cooking juices, skimming when the fat rises to the surface.

6. Arrange the chicken neatly on a serving platter. Leave covered.

7. Fry the ginger and mushroom slices in hot oil for 30 seconds. Add the reserved cooking juices from steaming the chicken, the lemon slivers, lemon juice, sugar and seasoning to taste then finally the grated lemon rind.

8. Pour over the chicken, cool and set aside to allow the flavours to blend. The sauce will set like a jelly.

9. Garnish with coriander leaves and scatter with slivers of pepper.

CANTONESE STIR-FRY CHICKEN WITH MUSHROOMS AND BAMBOO SHOOTS

SHUANG DONG JI QIU

Also known as Moo Goo Gai Pin in Cantonese, which means chicken slices with tiny mushrooms, try to find the straw mushrooms which are available in cans but if they are difficult to find then used sliced and quickly sautéed button mushrooms instead. Bak choy should not be confused with Chinese leaves. It looks much like Swiss chard, the stem is usually chopped up and used to give texture to the dish.

Serves 2–3

2 boneless chicken breasts, about 350 g/12 oz		
10 ml	cornflour (cornstarch), blended with 15 ml/1 tbsp water	2 tsp
	Salt and freshly ground black pepper	
15 ml	rice wine or dry sherry	1 tbsp
425 g	canned straw mushrooms, drained	15 oz
	1 bamboo shoot, sliced	
225 g	bak choy OR Chinese cabbage	8 oz
45 ml	oil	3 tbsp
150 ml	chicken stock or water	¼ pt/⅔ cup
5 ml	sugar	1 tsp
20 ml	cornflour (cornstarch), blended with 30 ml/2 tbsp water	4 tsp
	A little warmed sesame oil	

1. Using a very sharp knife, cut the chicken into fine slivers. Place in a bowl and add the blended cornflour, seasoning and rice wine or sherry. Mix well and set aside while preparing the other ingredients.

2. Place the drained mushrooms and sliced bamboo shoot in a bowl. Shred the bak choy or cabbage finely.

3. Heat the oil in a wok and when hot, stir-fry the chicken quickly, separating the pieces. This will take only 2–3 minutes. Scoop into a sieve over a bowl and collect the draining oil.

4. Pour the oil back into the wok. When hot, add the cabbage and cook for 20 seconds then add the bamboo shoot and mushrooms. Add the chicken stock or water and cook a further 30 seconds.

5. Add the sugar and blended cornflour to thicken slightly. Taste for seasoning, add the chicken and heat quickly.

6. Serve immediately drizzled with warmed sesame oil.

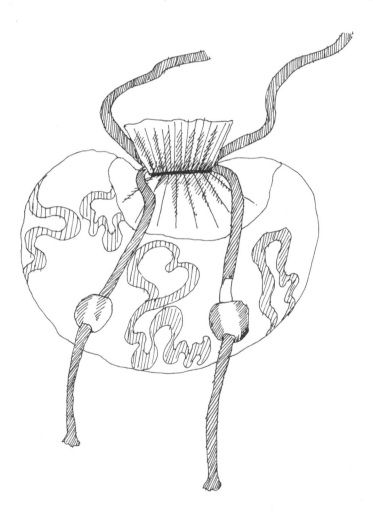

CHICKEN CUBES WITH KUNG PO SAUCE

KUNG PO JI DING

This has become one of the classic recipes on the Chinese menu which hails from the Szechuan region of Western China. Here I have used roasted peanuts which are very traditional, though many chefs use cashew nuts in their place.

Serves 3

	2 boneless chicken breasts, about 350 g/12 oz	
	1 egg white	
10 ml	cornflour (cornstarch)	2 tsp
	Salt	
30 ml	yellow salted beans	2 tbsp
15 ml	hoisin sauce	1 tbsp
5 ml	brown sugar	1 tsp
15 ml	rice wine or dry sherry	1 tbsp
15 ml	wine vinegar	1 tbsp
150 ml	stock or water	¼ pt/⅔ cup
	4 garlic cloves, crushed	
	2-3 dried chillies, broken into small pieces	
2.5 ml-5 ml	OR chilli powder	½-1 tsp
100 g	roasted peanuts, lightly crushed	4 oz/1 cup
45 ml	groundnut (peanut) or sunflower oil	3 tbsp

1. Cube the chicken into even-sized pieces. Lightly whisk the egg white, add the cornflour and salt then stir the chicken into this.

2. Mash the beans with the back of a spoon, add the hoisin sauce, sugar, rice wine or sherry, vinegar, stock or water and garlic.

3. Prepare the remaining ingredients.

4. Heat a wok then add the oil and when hot fry the chicken cubes for about 2 minutes until they are golden and cooked through. Turn constantly. Lift out of the wok or pan into a sieve over a bowl and collect the excess oil.

5. Heat the wok, pour in the oil from the bowl, and when hot, fry the pieces of chilli until turning in colour then add the bean sauce mixture and the chicken.

6. When hot, stir in most of the peanuts. Turn on to a hot serving dish and scatter the remaining peanuts on top.

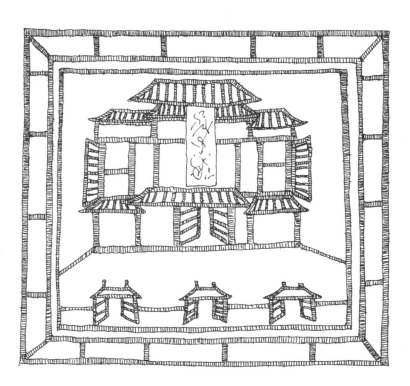

LETTUCE WRAP FROM THE PANDA RESTAURANT

SANG CHOY

owards the end of our meal and across the crowded Panda Restaurant, I spotted a group eating this lettuce wrap with great relish. We just had to return to try it and it was as delicious as it looked. Here is the recipe for this, the simplest of dishes.

Serves 6

	2 boneless chicken breasts, about 350 g/12 oz	
	4 Chinese dried mushrooms, soaked in warm water for 30 minutes	
	6 canned water chestnuts	
	2 garlic cloves, crushed	
30 ml	oil	2 tbsp
30 ml	light soy sauce	2 tbsp
5 ml	Szechuan peppercorns, dry-fried and crushed	1 tsp
	Salt and freshly ground black pepper	
	4 spring onions (scallions), finely chopped	
5 ml	sesame oil	1 tsp
	Oil for deep-frying	
50 g	bean thread noodles	2 oz
	TO SERVE:	
	Crisp lettuce leaves	
	Hoisin sauce	

1. Remove the skin from the breasts and chop the chicken as finely as possible with a sharp knife. A food processor will probably chop this too finely.

2. Drain the mushrooms, discard the stems and slice the caps finely. Drain the chestnuts and chop finely.

3. Fry the garlic in hot oil to release the flavour then add the chicken and stir-fry until it changes colour and looks cooked.

4. Add the mushrooms and water chestnuts, soy sauce and crushed peppercorns. Stir all the time.

5. Taste for seasoning and add some of the spring onions and sesame oil.

6. Heat the oil to 190°C/375°F and deep-fry the noodles until crisp, then drain and crush. They cook instantly if the oil is at the correct temperature.

7. Place the noodles in the base of a serving dish, top with the chicken mixture and remaining spring onions. Toss together thoroughly before serving.

8. Place the leaves of a Webbs or crisp lettuce on a large platter or basket.

9. Spoonfuls of the mixture are placed in the centre of each lettuce leaf which has first been lightly smeared with hoisin sauce. Roll each one into a neat parcel and eat at once.

CHILLI CHICKEN

LAZI JI

Use the red finger-shaped chillies for this recipe as they give an attractive appearance and good flavour to the finished dish. See page 35 for information on preparation of chillies.

Serves 4–5

4 boneless chicken breasts, about 550 g/1¼ lb		
5 ml	sugar	1 tsp
2–3 fresh chillies depending on size and hotness you prefer		
2 Brazil nuts or 4 shelled almonds		
1 stem lemon grass, root trimmed and lower 6 cm/2½ in sliced		
5 ml	fenugreek	1 tsp
2.5 cm	fresh ginger, peeled, sliced and cut into matchsticks	1 in
4–6 shallots or 1 red onion, thinly sliced		
3–4 garlic cloves, crushed		
60 ml	sunflower oil	4 tbsp
150 ml	chicken stock or water	¼ pt/⅔ cup
Salt		

GARNISH
3 spring onions (scallions), sliced

1. Remove the skin then cut each of the chicken breasts into 8 long finger-like pieces. Sprinkle with sugar and set aside whilst preparing the other ingredients.

2. Pound the chillies with the nuts, lemon grass, fenugreek and half the ginger, either in a pestle and mortar or food processor.

3. Pound the remaining ginger with the onions and garlic in the same way.

4. About 10 minutes before serving, heat the wok and then add the oil and stir-fry the spice mixture for 1–2 minutes then add the onion mixture and stir-fry again for a further 1–2 minutes.

5. Add the chicken pieces, turning in the spicy mixture until well coated.

6. Add the stock or water and salt to taste. Cover with a lid and cook for 4–5 minutes.

7. Transfer to a hot serving platter and garnish with slivers of spring onion.

SPICED CHICKEN DRUMSTICKS

WU XIAN JI TUI

*D*rumsticks cooked in this way are very succulent and moreish
and rather good on the barbecue, too. Prepare them ahead of
time and just place them on the barbecue to heat through for 3–4
minutes in a foil parcel to prevent the spicy, coated drumsticks from
over browning.

Serves 4, or more as part of a meal

	8 chicken drumsticks, skinned	
15 ml	sugar	1 tbsp
5 ml	five-spice powder	1 tsp
100 ml	rice wine or dry sherry	3½ fl oz/ 6½ tbsp
	2 sticks cinnamon	
30 ml	light soy sauce	2 tbsp
30 ml	dark soy sauce	2 tbsp
	Salt	
	GARNISH:	
	Cucumber slices	

1. Rub the drumsticks with sugar and set aside for 15 minutes
to draw the juices. Rub with five-spice powder.

2. Lightly oil a wok or frying pan (skillet) then place the
chicken drumsticks in this with the rice wine or sherry and cook over a
gentle heat until the wine or sherry has almost evaporated.

3. Add 200 ml/7 fl oz/scant 1 cup of water, the cinnamon
sticks, soy sauces and salt to taste. Bring to the boil then reduce the
heat to a simmer, turning the drumsticks frequently until quite tender.
This will take about 35 minutes. If the sauce evaporates, add a little
more hot water and wine or sherry.

4. Serve hot, warm or cold glazed with the syrupy sauce from
the bottom of the wok or pan. Garnish with sliced cucumber.

BEEF AND LAMB

STIR-FRY BEEF WITH OYSTER SAUCE

HAO YOU NIU ROU

little beef goes a long way when cut into paper-thin slices. In addition, it cooks speedily so this is perfect for an impressive last-minute dish. Add a little luxury and toss in 100 g/4 oz drained canned oysters at the same time as the sauce ingredients.

Serves 2–3, or more as part of a buffet

225 g	beef fillet	8 oz
30 ml	rice wine or dry sherry	2 tbsp
30 ml	oyster sauce	2 tbsp
15 ml	light soy sauce	1 tbsp
5 ml	dark brown sugar	1 tsp
	Salt and freshly ground black pepper	
45 ml	beef stock or water	3 tbsp
45 ml	oil	3 tbsp
1 cm	fresh ginger, peeled and finely shredded	½ in
	4 spring onions (scallions), finely shredded	
100 g	canned oysters, drained (optional)	4 oz
5 ml	cornflour (cornstarch), mixed to a paste with water	1 tsp

1. Use a very sharp knife to slice the beef into thin, even slices. Set aside on a plate sprinkled with the rice wine or sherry.

2. Blend the oyster sauce, soy sauce, sugar, seasoning and stock or water. Prepare the remaining ingredients.

3. When ready to cook, pour the juices from the beef into the sauce.

4. Warm the wok, add the oil and when hot stir-fry the beef slices for about 1 minute until the meat changes colour. Lift out on a draining spoon and keep warm.

5. Heat the savoury juices left in the wok. Add the ginger and most of the spring onions. Fry until wilted then add the beef, oysters if using, sauce mixture and cornflour to slightly thicken the sauce. Taste for seasoning.

6. Serve at once garnished with remaining spring onions.

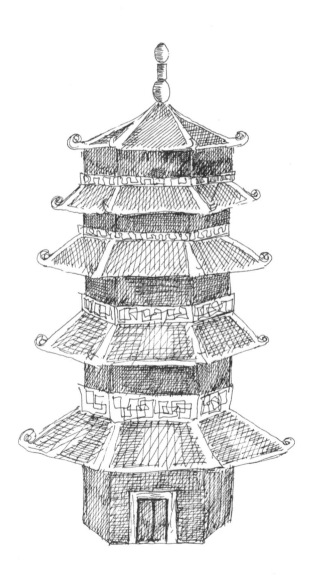

SPICED SHREDDED FRIED BEEF

GAN CHAO NIU SI

*I*n this recipe the beef should be cut into fine shreds. It is a good
  idea to place the piece of beef in the freezer for 30 minutes to firm
up first before cutting with a sharp knife.

Serves 2, or 4 as part of a meal

225 g	rump or fillet steak	8 oz
15 ml	light soy sauce	1 tbsp
15 ml	dark soy sauce	1 tbsp
15 ml	rice wine or sherry	1 tbsp
5 ml	dark brown or golden granulated sugar	1 tsp
	2 carrots, sliced as thinly as possible	
	1 stick celery, thinly sliced	
2.5 cm fresh ginger, peeled and shredded		1 in
	2–3 dried whole chillies OR	
5 ml	crushed chilli paste	1 tsp
60 ml	oil	4 tbsp
	Salt	

GARNISH:	
1 fresh chilli, deseeded and sliced	

1. Slice and shred the beef finely into even-sized matchstick-like pieces. Place in a bowl with the soy sauces, wine or sherry and sugar.

2. Prepare the carrots, celery and ginger. Break the whole chillies into pieces, if using, or measure out the crushed chilli, bearing in mind your guests' tolerance to spicy foods.

3. When ready to cook, heat the wok, add half the oil and when hot add the beef, stirring constantly. Cook for 1 minute then lift out into a bowl and keep warm.

4. Add the remaining oil and quickly fry the ginger, followed by chillies or crushed chilli and cook briefly over a high heat.

5. Add the carrot and celery slices for 1-2 minutes, stirring all the time, then return the beef and cooking juices to the pan. Season with salt, cover and cook for 30 seconds and serve garnished with sliced chilli.

GINGER BEEF WITH SNOW PEAS

SHI CAI CHAI NIU PIAN

Snow peas, a rather prettier name than mangetout, are available all the year round from East and Southern Africa in particular.
Serves 2-3, or more as part of a meal

225 g	fillet or rump steak	8 oz
5 ml	cornflour (cornstarch)	1 tsp
15 ml	rice wine or sherry	1 tbsp
15 ml	dark soy sauce	1 tbsp
	Salt and freshly ground black pepper	
2.5 cm	fresh ginger, peeled, finely sliced and shredded	1 in
100 g	mangetout	4 oz
45 ml	oil for frying	3 tbsp
5 ml	dark brown sugar	1 tsp
45 ml	stock or water	3 tbsp

1. Thinly slice the steak. Mix the cornflour, wine or sherry, soy sauce and seasoning. Spoon over the meat then mix well.

2. Prepare the ginger, mangetout and remaining ingredients.

3. When ready to cook, warm the wok, add the oil and when hot, quickly fry the shredded ginger for 30 seconds.

4. Quickly add the beef and toss constantly until it changes colour, about 30 seconds.

5. Now add the mangetout, sugar and stock or water. Toss well then cover for about 30 seconds when the mangetout will have taken on a rich jewel-like colour and the juices will have produced a rich sauce. Serve immediately seasoned with pepper.

BEEF WITH GREEN PEPPERS AND BLACK BEAN SAUCE

SI JIAO NIU ROU

his is a stunning combination of textures and flavours. Choose good quality beef when stir-frying such as rump, sirloin or fillet. Serves 3, or more as part of a meal

275 g	rump, sirloin or fillet steak	10 oz
	1 egg white, lightly whisked	
15 ml	cornflour (cornstarch)	1 tbsp
15 ml	light soy sauce	1 tbsp
	Salt and freshly ground black pepper	
45 ml	salted black beans	3 tbsp
	1 good-size green (bell) pepper, deseeded and cubed	
60 ml	oil	4 tbsp
	2 garlic cloves, crushed	
1 cm	fresh ginger, peeled and shredded	½ in
5 ml	dark brown sugar	1 tsp
100 ml	stock or water	3½ fl oz/6½ tbsp

1. Thinly slice the beef then cut into long strips. Blend the egg white, cornflour, soy sauce and seasoning. Add the beef strips.

2. Rinse the black beans and crush, if liked. Prepare the pepper and remaining ingredients.

3. Heat a wok, add 30 ml/2 tbsp of the oil and when hot fry the green pepper until brightly coloured and only slightly softened. Lift out of the pan with the cooking juices.

4. Quickly fry the garlic and ginger in the remaining oil until softened then add the beef strips in the marinade and the black beans. Fry over a high heat, stirring constantly, for 1 minute. Add the sugar and stock or water, return the peppers to the wok and serve when really hot.

LAMB IN LETTUCE PARCELS FROM THE KAIFENG

YANG ROU SHENG CAI BAO

ariations on the Peking duck theme, this is a stunning way to serve a modest shoulder of lamb. Ask the butcher to bone out the shoulder for you. The bones can be used to make a stock. The shoulder is first marinated in the spices, steamed and then rested before deep-frying to crisp up the skin.

Serves 6

	1 boned shoulder of lamb, about 1.25 kg/3 lb	
2.5 ml	black peppercorns or Szechuan peppercorns	½ tsp
5 ml	five-spice powder	1 tsp
15 ml	clear honey	1 tbsp
15 ml	dark soy sauce	1 tbsp
30 ml	light soy sauce	2 tbsp
15 ml	rice wine or dry sherry	1 tbsp
2 cm	fresh ginger, peeled and shredded	1 in
	1 bunch spring onions (scallions), cut into short lengths	
	Oil for deep-frying	

TO SERVE:
Hoisin and plum sauces
1 cucumber, cut into thin strips
1 bunch spring onions (scallions), shredded
1 or 2 lettuces, leaves separated, washed and dried

1. Wipe the lamb and set aside.

2. Crush the peppercorns and mix with the five-spice powder, honey, soy sauces and rice wine or sherry.

3. Place the ginger and spring onions in the centre of the joint. Tie into a roll. Place in a bowl and rub the spice mixture all over the meat. Marinate for at least 3 hours.

4. Place on a large plate which will fit into a steamer and steam for 2 hours until tender or cook in the oven as directed in the recipe for Aromatic Crispy Duck (see page 100).

5. Drain on a trivet for 3–4 hours.

6. Just before serving, assemble all the accompaniments.

7. Heat the oil to 190°/375°F and carefully lower the lamb into the fat to fry and crisp for 10 minutes.

8. Remove the crisp skin and chop the meat into neat pieces. Serve by smearing the leaves with the sauces, placing cucumber and shreds of spring onion and meat in each leaf and rolling up neatly. It does help to slightly flatten the leaves if they are especially curly, so that you can make a neater parcel for eating.

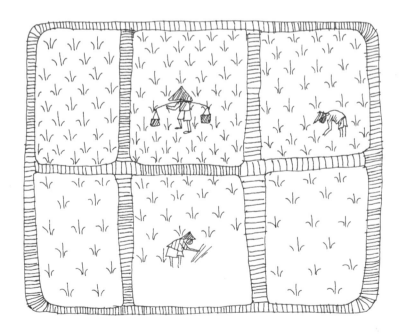

STIR-FRIED LAMB WITH LEEKS

CONG BAO YANG ROU

amb dishes are popular in the northern region, where huge flocks of sheep graze the large expanses of grassland.
Serves 4 as part of a meal

350 g	lean lamb from leg or neck fillet	12 oz
1.5 ml	five-spice powder	¼ tsp
15 ml	dark soy sauce	1 tbsp
15 ml	gin	1 tbsp
15 ml	sesame oil	1 tbsp
	2 leeks	
	2 garlic cloves	
45 ml	groundnut (peanut) oil	3 tbsp
60 ml	chicken stock or water	4 tbsp
	Salt and freshly ground black pepper	

1. Slice the meat thinly across the grain and sprinkle with five-spice powder. Place in a bowl with the soy sauce, gin and sesame oil and leave to marinate.

2. Trim the root from the leeks, wash and shred finely.

3. Fry the garlic in hot oil in a wok without browning. Turn the heat to high and add the lamb and marinade and stir constantly for 2 minutes.

4. Now add the shredded leeks and chicken stock or water and cook over a high heat, covered with a lid, for a further 1 minute then taste for seasoning and serve at once.

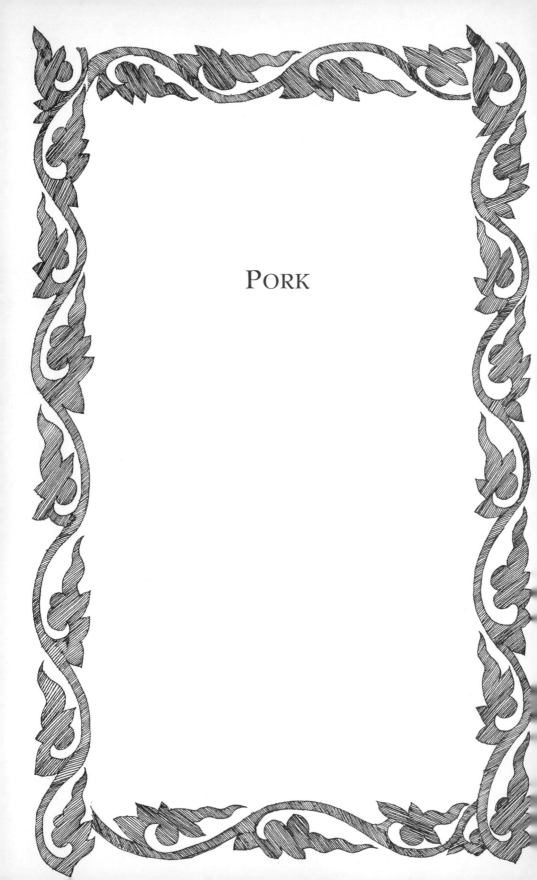

PORK

ROAST PORK FILLET

MI ZI CHAR SUI

A favourite food, this is often served on its own as part of a meal or can be used as one of the ingredients, see the Red-cooked Aubergine recipe (see page 156).

Serves 3–4

450 g	pork fillet	1 lb
	MARINADE:	
15 ml	hoisin sauce	1 tbsp
15 ml	rice wine or dry sherry	1 tbsp
15 ml	clear honey	1 tbsp
15 ml	dark soy sauce	1 tbsp
	Salt and freshly ground black pepper	

1. Trim any of the fine connecting skin from the fillet.

2. Spoon the marinade ingredients into a glass or stainless steel dish and mix well.

3. Place the fillet in the marinade and turn to coat. Marinate for about 2 hours.

4. Set on a trivet over a roasting tin with water just to cover the bottom of the tin.

5. Roast in a preheated hot oven at 220°C/425°F/gas 7 and cook for 30 minutes. The juices run clear when tested with a skewer. Remove from the oven. Serve either hot or cold.

BRAISED LION HEADS

SHI ZI TOU

*T*hese are large meat balls, significantly larger than the normal meat balls we would make. They are so called because the meat ball on the serving platter resembles the head of the lion and the noodles or shredded cabbage the mane.

Serves 3–4

450 g	lean pork, minced with a little fat	1 lb
	6 canned water chestnuts, finely chopped	
1 cm	fresh ginger, peeled and finely chopped	½ in
	½ small onion, finely chopped	
30 ml	light soy sauce	2 tbsp
	Salt and freshly ground black pepper	
	A little beaten egg to bind	
30 ml	seasoned cornflour (cornstarch)	2 tbsp
90 ml	groundnut (peanut) or sunflower oil	6 tbsp
300 ml	chicken stock	½ pt/1¼ cups
2.5 ml	sugar	½ tsp
100 g	each Chinese leaves and spinach, shredded	4 oz
	OR	
50 g	bean thread noodles, soaked in warm water	2 oz

1. Mix the pork, water chestnuts, ginger, onion, half the soy sauce and seasoning together. Bind with sufficient beaten egg then form into 8 balls with wetted hands.

2. Spread the seasoned cornflour on a sheet of greaseproof paper and toss the meat balls in some of this, then make a paste with the remaining cornflour with water and reserve.

3. Fry the meat balls in hot oil to brown all over then transfer to a clean pan or flameproof casserole.

4. Heat the stock and pour over the meat balls. Add the sugar, seasoning and remaining soy sauce. Cover and simmer for 25–30 minutes then transfer the meat balls to a dish and keep warm.

5. Add the cabbage and spinach or the soaked noodles to the liquid in the casserole and cook rapidly for 2–3 minutes, adding some extra stock if necessary. Lift the vegetables or noodles from the pan with a draining spoon and arrange on a serving platter. Top with the meat balls.

6. Slightly thicken the sauce with the reserved cornflour paste. Taste for seasoning and pour over the meat balls just before serving.

TWICE-COOKED PORK

HUI GUO ROU

A *very popular and much loved pork dish from Szechuan, the pork is first cooked in water until tender and then sliced and tossed with a highly spiced mixture which is typical of the Szechuan cuisine.*

Serves 6

1 kg belly pork, bones and rind removed 2¼ lb		
60 ml	preserved black beans	4 tbsp
15 ml	hot soy bean paste or Szechuan sauce	1 tbsp
30 ml	light soy sauce	2 tbsp
15 ml	tomato purée (paste)	1 tbsp
15 ml	hoisin sauce	1 tbsp
10 ml	chilli sauce or 1-2 red chillies, deseeded and pounded	2 tsp
15 ml	dark brown sugar	1 tbsp
60 ml	oil	4 tbsp
	2 garlic cloves, crushed	
1 cm	fresh ginger, peeled and shredded	½ in
60 ml	chicken stock	4 tbsp
30 ml	rice wine or sherry	2 tbsp
225 g	canned bamboo shoots, drained and sliced	8 oz
	A little sesame oil	
	4 spring onions (scallions), thinly sliced	

1. Place the pork in a piece in a pan with water just to cover. Bring to the boil. Cover and simmer for 30–40 minutes until tender when tested with a skewer.

2. Lift out, cool then cut into fine slices and reserve.

3. Rinse the beans and mash with the back of a wooden spoon in a bowl. Blend the soy bean paste or Szechuan sauce with the soy sauce, tomato purée, hoisin sauce, chilli sauce and sugar.

4. Prepare the garlic, ginger and remaining ingredients.

5. When ready to cook, heat the wok, add the oil and when hot, fry the garlic, ginger and mashed beans until they give off a rich aroma.

6. Add the cooked pork and the mixture of sauces, tossing so that the meat slices are coated with the mixture. Add the stock and wine or sherry and a little extra water if the sauce is too thick.

7. Cook gently for 4–5 minutes, increase the heat and add the bamboo shoots, sesame oil and spring onions. Cook for 1 minute and serve immediately with plain boiled rice.

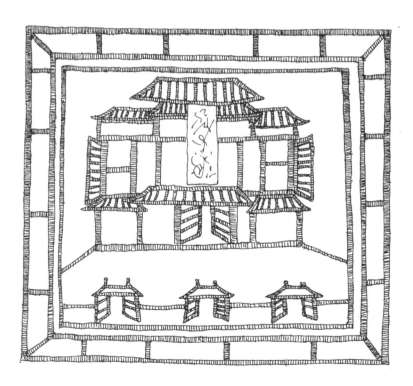

SWEET AND SOUR PORK

GU LUO ROU

*C*antonese chefs were the first to emigrate and introduced this
renowned and ever-popular pork dish wherever they went.
Traditionally, the Chinese use good quality belly pork as they like to have
a balance of lean and fat, but you can of course use fillet of pork if you
prefer.

Serves 6

550 g	belly pork, boned and rind removed or pork fillet	1¼ lb
15 ml	dark soy sauce	1 tbsp
15 ml	rice wine or sherry	1 tbsp
50 g	cornflour (cornstarch)	2 oz/½ cup
	4 Chinese dried mushrooms, soaked in warm water for 30 minutes	
	½ red (bell) pepper, deseeded and cubed	
	½ green (bell) pepper, deseeded and cubed	
	1 small carrot, sliced thinly	
	1 small onion, cut into thin wedges	
450 g	canned pineapple cubes in light syrup, drained and halved	1 lb
	2 garlic cloves, crushed	
1 cm	fresh ginger, peeled and finely shredded	½ in
200 ml	water	7 fl oz/scant 1 cup
45–60 ml	sugar	3–4 tbsp
60 ml	red wine vinegar	4 tbsp
15 ml	light soy sauce	1 tbsp
5 ml	tomato purée (paste)	1 tsp
	Salt	
450 ml	oil for frying	¾ pt/2 cups

1. Cut the pork into neat cubes then beat lightly with a rolling pin to tenderise. Place in a bowl with the soy sauce and rice wine or sherry then mix well.

2. Reserve 15 ml/1 tbsp of cornflour to thicken the sauce. Spread a sheet of greaseproof paper on a large plate or tray and cover with the remainder of the cornflour. The drained pork pieces will be coated in this just before frying, but do this only when ready to start cooking.

3. Drain the mushrooms and reserve the liquid. Discard the stalks and slice the caps thinly.

4. Add the mushrooms to the cubes of red and green peppers, the carrots, the onion and the halved pineapple cubes in a bowl.

5. Blend a little of the pineapple juice with the reserved cornflour to a thin paste.

6. Prepare the garlic and ginger. Pour the remaining pineapple juice into a measuring jug and make up to 300 ml/½ pt/1¼ cups with water. Add the sugar, vinegar, soy sauce and tomato purée with the marinade from the meat. Add salt to taste.

7. When ready to start cooking, heat the oil to 190°C/375°F. Coat the pieces of pork in cornflour and fry in a few batches for about 6–8 minutes until the pork is crisp and cooked through. Drain well and keep warm.

8. Spoon 45 ml/3 tbsp of the oil into a clean wok or pan, add the garlic and ginger and cook for 1 minute then add the prepared vegetables and toss well over medium heat for 2–3 minutes.

9. Add the pineapple and water mixture and allow to come to the boil then stir in the cornflour paste to thicken slightly.

10. Add the crispy pork, taste and adjust the seasoning and serve at once with rice.

PORK AND CLOUD EAR PANCAKES

MU-SHU-RON

*n unusual combination of pork and scrambled eggs flavoured
with cloud ears and lily stems, this dish has its origins in Northern
China, though it has become very popular wherever it has been
introduced. It is served as a filling for the Mandarin pancakes which are
usually associated with Peking duck. You can now buy the pancakes
from large supermarkets as well as from oriental stores.*
  Serves 4

225 g	finely minced (ground) pork	8 oz
8 dried tiger lily buds, soaked in warm water for 30 minutes		
4 pieces wood ears, soaked in warm water for 30 minutes		
1 cm	fresh ginger, peeled and finely shredded	½ in
3 eggs, lightly beaten		
60 ml	groundnut (peanut) or sunflower oil	4 tbsp
100 g	canned bamboo shoots, sliced	4 oz
2 spring onions (scallions), finely shredded		
15 ml	dark soy sauce	1 tbsp
5 ml	dark brown sugar	1 tsp
60 ml	chicken stock or water	4 tbsp
15 ml	rice wine or sherry	1 tbsp
Freshly ground black pepper		
A little sesame oil		
SAUCE:		
30 ml	oil	2 tbsp
100 g	yellow bean sauce	4 oz
30 ml	sugar	2 tbsp
10 Mandarin Pancakes (see page 112)		

1. Set the pork on one side. Drain then trim the hard tips from the lily buds and the wood ears. Cut into small pieces.

2. Fry the ginger shreds in half the hot oil in a non-stick pan without browning, then stir in the eggs and lightly scramble. Turn out into a bowl.

3. Heat the remaining oil, add the pork and stir constantly until the meat changes colour. Add the bamboo shoots, lily buds and wood ears and continue cooking for 2 minutes.

4. Add the spring onions, soy sauce, sugar, stock, rice wine or sherry, pepper and sesame oil.

5. Finally, stir in the scrambled egg mixture. The mixture should be fairly firm.

6. To make the sauce, heat the oil and fry the bean sauce for 1–2 minutes. Add sugar to taste and cook until the sugar dissolves.

7. Serve spoonfuls of the egg mixture on Mandarin pancakes rolled up and dipped in a yellow bean sauce.

RED-COOKED AUBERGINE WITH ROAST PORK

YU HSIANG GAIZI

nother all time favourite from the Panda Restaurant which specialises in Szechuan food. The aubergine is salted to remove the bitter juices. Rinse then dry thoroughly before deep-frying.
Serves 4, or more as part of a buffet

2 aubergines (eggplants), about 550 g/1¼ lb		
Oil for deep-frying		
4 Chinese dried mushrooms, soaked in water for 30 minutes		
275 g	canned bamboo shoots, sliced	10 oz
200 g	cooked roast pork	7 oz
45 ml	groundnut (peanut) or sunflower oil	3 tbsp
2 garlic cloves, crushed		
60–90 ml	chicken stock or mushroom soaking liquid	4–6 tbsp
60–90 ml	Szechuan sauce	4–6 tbsp
Salt and freshly ground black pepper		
1 red chilli, deseeded and finely sliced		

1. Trim the ends from the aubergines and cut into neat dice. Sprinkle with salt and leave 30 minutes, then drain off the juices, rinse and dry on kitchen paper.

2. Heat the oil to 190°C/375°F and deep-fry the aubergines in two batches. Drain on kitchen paper.

3. Drain the mushrooms, discard the stalks and slice the caps thinly. Reserve the soaking juices. Cut the bamboo shoots into matchstick-like pieces and the slices of pork in the same way.

4. Heat the oil in a wok and fry the garlic to release its flavour without browning. Add the Szechuan sauce and fry quickly then add the mushrooms, bamboo shoots, aubergine and pork pieces. Cook together, tossing well. Add the stock. Cook for 2 minutes then taste and adjust the seasoning. Serve at once garnished with thinly sliced chilli.

SHREDDED PORK WITH SZECHUAN PICKLED VEGETABLE

ZHA CAI ROU SI

he pickled vegetable is highly salted and so must be well rinsed before use in this or any recipe. Any leftover vegetable from the can may be transferred to a glass jar, covered closely with clingfilm and a lid and kept in the refrigerator for several weeks.

Serves 4–6

450 g	pork fillet	1 lb
15 ml	dark soy sauce	1 tbsp
175 g	canned Szechuan pickled vegetable	6 oz
45 ml	groundnut (peanut) oil	3 tbsp
10 ml	dark brown sugar	2 tsp
30 ml	rice wine or sherry	2 tbsp
	Freshly ground black pepper	
	A little sesame oil, heated	
	A few toasted sesame seeds	
	1 red chilli, deseeded and sliced	

1. Slice the pork thinly and then into the finest strips. Mix in a bowl with the soy sauce.

2. Rinse the salt from the pickled vegetable, dry and shred finely.

3. Prepare the remaining ingredients.

4. When ready to start cooking, heat the wok, add the oil and when hot, add the pork, turning for 3–4 minutes until the pork changes colour.

5. Add the shredded vegetable and toss well, then add the sugar and rice wine or sherry.

6. Add pepper to taste and spoon on to a platter. Drizzle with warm sesame oil and scatter with sesame seeds. Garnish with the sliced chilli.

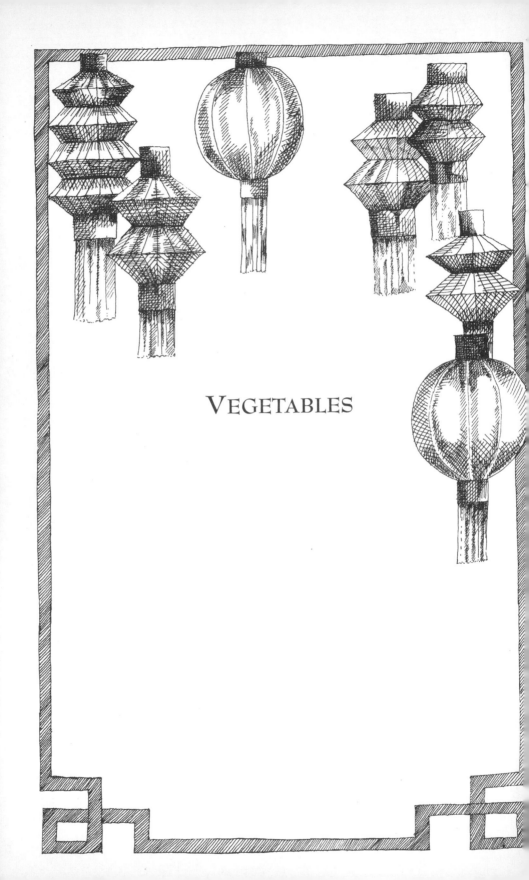

VEGETABLES

VEGETARIAN FOUR TREASURES

CHAO SU SI BAO

This is a delightful name for a simple stir-fry of vegetables. Different vegetable combinations can be used, paying attention to texture, colour and complementary flavours.

Serves 4–6

	6 Chinese dried mushrooms, soaked in water for 30 minutes	
	2 garlic cloves	
1 cm	fresh ginger, peeled and shredded	½ in
150 g	mangetout	6 oz
100 g	baby sweetcorn, cut in half if liked	4 oz
	12 canned water chestnuts	
45 ml	groundnut (peanut) or sunflower oil	3 tbsp
15 ml	light soy sauce	1 tbsp
10 ml	cornflour (cornstarch) blended to a thin paste with water	2 tsp
	Salt and freshly ground black pepper	

1. Drain the water from the mushrooms and reserve. Discard the tough stems and thinly slice the caps. Prepare the remaining vegetables and place on a tray next to the cooker.

2. Heat the wok, add the oil and when hot fry the garlic and ginger for 30 seconds, stirring.

3. Add the mushroom slices, mangetout, sweetcorn and chestnuts, tossing well, then after 1 minute add 90 ml/6 tbsp of the mushroom soaking water. Cover and steam for 1 minute.

4. Add the soy sauce, and at the last minute thicken slightly with the blended cornflour. Taste for seasoning and serve at once whilst the vegetables are still crisp and jewel-like in colour.

BUDDHIST MONK'S VEGETABLE CREATION

LO HAN ZHAI MATAR PANEER

*I*ts name means the 'Buddhist's vegetable ensemble for the gods'. The vegetarian Buddhist monks spend long hours in prayer and additionally gain inspiration in interesting and diverse ways of cooking and serving vegetables. This is their most famous recipe. The list of ingredients may seem formidable and sound complicated, but I can assure you that it is extraordinarily delicious and well worth the effort.
Serves 4-6

	6 Chinese dried mushrooms, soaked in water for 30 minutes	
	12 lily buds, soaked in water for 30 minutes	
25 g	wood ears, soaked in water for 30 minutes	1 oz
25 g	bean thread noodles, soaked in water	1 oz
25 g	Chinese hair seaweed, soaked in water for 30 minutes (optional)	1 oz
175 g	canned lotus root	6 oz
225 g	Chinese cabbage or bak choy, shredded	8 oz
150 g	broccoli florets	5 oz
150 g	cauliflower florets	5 oz
100 g	mangetout	4 oz
100 g	bean sprouts	4 oz
	2 carrots, thinly sliced	
	1 red (bell) pepper, deseeded and cubed	
	1 green (bell) pepper, deseeded and cubed	
225 g	fresh beancurd or fried beancurd	8 oz
90 ml	groundnut (peanut) or sunflower oil	6 tbsp

	1 garlic clove, crushed	
1.5 litres	vegetable or chicken stock	2½ pts/6 cups
60 ml	light soy sauce	4 tbsp
	Salt and freshly ground black pepper	
	Sesame oil	

1. Drain the mushrooms, discard the hard stems and thinly slice the caps. Reserve the soaking liquid.

2. Drain the lily buds and wood ears, discard the tough ends then tie each lily bud into a knot.

3. Drain the water from hair seaweed, if using. Leave the bean thread noodles in water until required and cut into shorter lengths with scissors.

4. Slice the lotus root into pieces about twice the thickness of a 50 pence piece.

5. Prepare the fresh vegetables as suggested. Choose a different selection if you have others to hand.

6. Cut the beancurd into 6 or 8 cubes, blot dry on kitchen paper and set aside, or use the fried beancurd.

7. Heat 45 ml/3 tbsp of the oil in a wok and stir-fry the mushrooms, lily buds, wood ears and hair seaweed for 1 minute. Turn out of the wok and reheat, adding half the remaining oil.

8. Gently fry the cubes of fresh beancurd, turning carefully, until brown on all sides. Lift on to a plate with the fried mushrooms. Fry the lotus root slices and add to the beancurd and mushrooms. If using the ready fried beancurd, add later.

9. Add the remaining oil and fry the garlic to flavour the oil. Now add the fresh vegetables and stir-fry for 2–3 minutes, tossing all the time, then add the stock, soy sauce, seasoning and fried mushrooms plus the drained noodles and fried beancurd.

10. Bring to the boil and simmer for 20 minutes. Taste for seasoning and drizzle a little sesame oil over the top before taking to the table. Serve with plenty of freshly cooked rice.

MA PO'S BEANCURD
IN HOT SAUCE

MA PO DAO FU

*H*ot and spicy, this is a typical Szechuan blend of flavours. Though traditionally made with pork you can equally well use prawns or firm fish but add just before the peas and spring onions so that the fish is not overcooked.

Serves 3–4, or more as part of a meal

225 g	minced (ground) pork or prawns or cubes of cod or haddock	8 oz
15 ml	hot bean sauce	1 tbsp
5 ml	dark soy sauce	1 tsp
5 ml	dark brown sugar	1 tsp
300 g	beancurd, cut into small dice	12 oz
45 ml	groundnut (peanut) or sunflower oil	3 tbsp
	2 garlic cloves, crushed	
1 cm	fresh ginger, peeled and finely shredded	½ in
	1–2 red chilli peppers, deseeded and thinly sliced	
100 g	canned pickled vegetable	4 oz
120 ml	stock or water	4 fl oz/½ cup
5 ml	Szechuan peppercorns, dry-fried and crushed	1 tsp
15 ml	hoisin sauce	1 tbsp
50 g	mangetout or fresh or frozen peas	2 oz
	4 spring onions (scallions), shredded	
5 ml	cornflour (cornstarch) mixed to a paste with water	1 tsp
	Salt and freshly ground black pepper	
	Sesame oil	

1. Mix the pork with the hot bean sauce, soy sauce and sugar. If using fish, keep separate.

2. Prepare the beancurd and the remaining ingredients.

3. Heat the wok, add the oil and when hot fry the garlic, ginger and chillies for 30 seconds then stir in the pork mixture and cook for 2 minutes until the meat has changed colour and texture.

4. Add the pickled vegetable and stock or water then the peppercorns, hoisin sauce and finally the beancurd. Take care to stir gently to prevent the beancurd breaking up.

5. Cook for 10 minutes if using pork or 5 minutes if fish is being used. The fish is added at this stage. Add the mangetout or peas and most of the spring onions.

6. Cook for a further 3 minutes then thicken with the blended cornflour. Season to taste.

7. Drizzle the top with sesame oil and garnish with the remaining spring onions before serving.

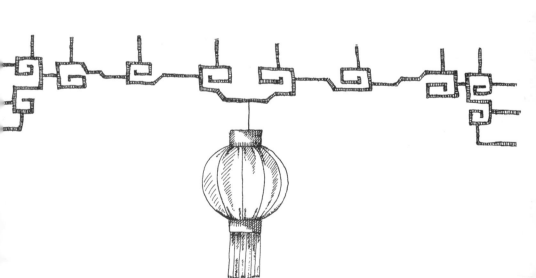

STIR-FRIED MUSTARD GREENS WITH OYSTER SAUCE

HAO YOU GAILAN

ustard greens look remarkably like Swiss chard, but any cabbage can be used or indeed the winter-season curly kale.
Serves 4 as part of a menu

	6 Chinese dried mushrooms, soaked in water for 30 minutes	
450 g	mustard greens, leafy cabbage or kale	1 lb
1 cm	fresh ginger, peeled and shredded	½ in
45 ml	groundnut (peanut) or sunflower oil	3 tbsp
30 ml	oyster sauce	2 tbsp
5 ml	sugar	1 tsp
	Salt and freshly ground black pepper	

1. Drain the mushrooms and reserve the soaking liquid. Discard the stems and slice the caps.

2. Tear the leaves from the stems of cabbage. Cut the stems into neat, chunky pieces. If using kale you might need to lightly parboil the stems first so that the cooking time can be kept to a minimum.

3. Heat the wok, add the oil and when hot quickly fry the ginger to flavour the oil. Toss in the cabbage stems and after 30 seconds the mushroom slices, then the leaves and the oyster sauce.

4. Add 45 ml/3 tbsp of the mushroom soaking liquid and the sugar. Keep cooking over a high heat for 30 seconds until the liquid has almost evaporated. Taste for seasoning and serve.

SPICY SWEET AND SOUR CABBAGE

TANG CU PAN BAICAI

Even the humble cabbage gets a facelift in this recipe with a tantalising sweet and sour flavour plus a little after-kick from the Szechuan peppercorns and chillies.

Serves 4–6

450 g	Chinese leaves	1 lb
15 ml	salt	1 tbsp
100 ml	white wine 3½ fl oz/6½ tbsp or cider vinegar	
30 ml	light brown or golden granulated sugar	2 tbsp
5 ml	Szechuan peppercorns, dry-fried and crushed	1 tsp
2.5 cm	fresh ginger, peeled and shredded	1 in
30 ml	groundnut (peanut) oil	2 tbsp
2.5 ml	4 dried chilli peppers, crushed, OR chilli powder	½ tsp
	1 red (bell) pepper, deseeded and cut into slivers	

1. Remove any discoloured leaves then shred the rest of the cabbage into strips across the stem. Place in a bowl, sprinkle with salt and set aside for about an hour to allow the juices to be drawn from the leaves.

2. Squeeze the leaves to extract the moisture and place the shreds into a serving dish. Meanwhile, heat the vinegar and sugar, stirring until the sugar has dissolved. Cool and pour over the leaves with the crushed peppercorns. Prepare the ginger.

3. Heat the oil and fry the ginger, tossing well, then add the crushed chillies to bring out the flavour, without allowing it to brown.

4. Finally, add the slivers of fresh red pepper and spoon on to the cabbage. Toss well together, cool, then cover with clingfilm and leave to stand for about 1 hour before serving.

SNOW PEAS AND STRAW MUSHROOMS

XUE DAO HUI CAO GU

uite as delicious as it sounds! The mangetout are available fresh almost all the year round, but as far as I know the straw mushrooms are available only in cans. Of course, we can now buy the delightful chestnut or oyster mushrooms which you may prefer.

Serves 4–6

225 g	mangetout	8 oz
425 g	canned straw mushrooms, drained	15 oz
	OR	
150 g	chestnut or oyster mushrooms	5 oz
30 ml	vegetable stock or water	2 tbsp
30 ml	oyster sauce	2 tbsp
15 ml	light soy sauce	1 tbsp
15 ml	rice wine or sherry	1 tbsp
30 ml	groundnut (peanut) or sunflower oil	2 tbsp
	1 garlic clove, crushed	
	Salt and freshly ground black pepper	
	A little sesame oil, warmed (optional)	

1. Set the mangetout on one side. Drain the canned mushrooms or if using the fresh mushrooms trim and discard the ends of the stems. Slice neatly.

2. Blend the stock or water, oyster and soy sauces with the rice wine or sherry.

3. Heat the wok, add the oil and fry the garlic without browning to flavour the oil. Add the mushrooms followed by the mangetout and toss well for 30 seconds.

4. Pour in the sauce mixture and cook for 1 minute only so that the peas remain crunchy. Taste for seasoning, turn on to a serving plate and drizzle with a little warmed sesame oil if liked.

FRENCH BEANS WITH BAMBOO SHOOTS AND CHICKEN OIL

JI YOU DONGSUN

*C*hicken oil may seem a curious addition to us but once tasted you will appreciate just how it gives this stir-fry another dimension. Frequently a chicken has two little pockets of fat at the vent. These and any other fat can be slowly rendered down to oil either in a slow oven or gently in a frying pan. Cool then strain into a screw-top jar and store in the refrigerator.

Serves 4, or more as part of a meal

225 g	extra fine beans	8 oz
225 g	canned bamboo shoots, drained	8 oz
1 cm	fresh ginger, peeled and crushed in a garlic press	½ in
30 ml	groundnut (peanut) or sunflower oil	2 tbsp
60 ml	vegetable stock or water	4 tbsp
2.5 ml	cornflour (cornstarch) blended to a thin paste with water	½ tsp
5–10 ml	chicken oil (see above)	1–2 tsp
	Salt and freshly ground black pepper	

1. Prepare the beans and bamboo shoots. Cut into bite-sized pieces. Prepare the ginger.

2. When ready to cook, heat the wok, add the oil and when hot fry the ginger without browning to add flavour to the oil. Increase the heat, toss in the beans and bamboo shoots and keep moving until the beans are a bright emerald colour.

3. Add the stock and then the cornflour mixture to make a light glaze for the vegetables.

4. Add the rendered chicken oil and seasoning to taste. Serve immediately.

CANTONESE STIR-FRY VEGETABLES

SU SHI JIN

*T*his richly coloured vegetable selection reflects the sunny climes of China's southern region. Use tiny fresh button mushrooms if you like. Do not peel, just trim the stalk, rinse with cold water and use at once.

Serves 6

15 ml	light soy sauce	1 tbsp
15 ml	oyster sauce	1 tbsp
15 ml	rice wine or dry sherry	1 tbsp
1.5 ml	sugar	¼ tsp
45 ml	water	3 tbsp
1 cm	fresh ginger, peeled and chopped	½ in
30 ml	groundnut (peanut) or sunflower oil	2 tbsp
175 g	mangetout	6 oz
425 g	canned straw mushrooms, drained	15 oz
225 g	baby sweetcorn, sliced in half	8 oz
	1 small red (bell) pepper, deseeded and cut into diamond-shaped pieces	
	1 small green (bell) pepper, deseeded and cut into diamond-shaped pieces	
	Freshly ground black pepper	
	A little sesame oil	

1. Blend the soy and oyster sauces with the rice wine or sherry, sugar and water. Prepare the ginger.

2. In a wok, fry the ginger in the oil for a few seconds. Add the mangetout and stir-fry for 30 seconds. Add the mushrooms, sweetcorn and peppers and cook a further minute, stirring constantly.

3. Add the sauce and season with pepper. Cover and cook for 30 seconds. Turn off the heat and stir in the sesame oil. Serve at once.

STIR-FRY MIXED VEGETABLES

CHAO SHI CAI

o cut carrots into flower shapes, slice them into 7.5 cm/3 in chunks. Cut 3 or 4 V-shaped notches lengthways around the edge of each chunk. Then slice them ready to use.

Serves 4–6

45 ml	groundnut (peanut) or sunflower oil	3 tbsp
	1 garlic clove, crushed	
175 g	carrots, cut into flower shapes	6 oz
100–175 g	mangetout	4–6 oz
	15 canned water chestnuts, drained and halved horizontally	
100 g	spinach or Chinese leaves, torn or shredded	4 oz
100 g	cooked prawns	4 oz
30 ml	stock or water	2 tbsp
	Salt and freshly ground black pepper	

GARNISH:

Spring onion (scallion) slivers
or a few leaves of coriander (cilantro)

1. Heat the oil in a warm wok, add the garlic and cook over a low heat without browning.

2. Add the carrots, stirring constantly, and cook over a high heat for 2–3 minutes.

3. Add the mangetout and the water chestnuts, spinach or Chinese cabbage and the prawns. Do not overcook.

4. Spoon in the stock. Season to taste with salt and pepper and serve at once garnished with spring onions or coriander.

SPICY SZECHUAN-STYLE AUBERGINE

YU XIANG QIEZI

his is a marvellous vegetable dish which is almost a meal in itself and can be served equally well either hot or cold. Remember to adjust the amount of chilli paste to suit you and your guests. You can also use a ready prepared hot and spicy Szechuan stir-fry sauce instead of the chilli paste, which is excellent.

Serves 4, or more as part of a meal

2 aubergines (eggplants), about 550 g/1¼ lb		
15 ml	salt	1 tbsp
15–30 ml	chilli paste	1–2 tbsp
1–2 garlic cloves, crushed		
15 ml	dark soy sauce	1 tbsp
10 ml	light soy sauce	2 tsp
15 ml	rice vinegar	1 tbsp
5 ml	soft dark brown sugar	1 tsp
75–90 ml	sunflower oil	5–6 tbsp
5 ml	chilli powder	1 tsp
15 ml	rice wine or dry sherry	1 tbsp
150 ml	water	¼ pt/⅔ cup
Salt and freshly ground black pepper		

GARNISH:	
A few toasted sesame seeds	

1. Trim the ends from the aubergines and then cut through lengthwise. Slice each half into three lengthwise and then across into chunks. Place on a large plate and sprinkle with salt. Set aside for 15–20 minutes then rinse away the bitter juices and dry on kitchen paper.

2. Blend the chilli paste to your taste with the garlic, soy sauces, vinegar and sugar.

3. Heat the wok, add the oil and when hot add the aubergine chunks, chilli powder and rice wine or sherry all at once. Keep stirring till the chunks of aubergine are beginning to turn a little brown, then add the water. Season to taste.

4. Cover and steam for 2–3 minutes then remove the lid and pour in the spicy sauce mixture. Cook for 2 minutes then turn on to a serving dish and scatter with sesame seeds before serving.

HOT AND SOUR CUCUMBERS

SUNA LA CHIN GUA

he hot sweet and sour flavours added to the crunch of the cucumber pieces is a stunning combination. Any leftovers keep well in a closed container in the refrigerator. This is excellent to serve with pork or prawn dishes.

Serves 6–8

	2 cucumbers, about 350 g/12 oz each	
30 ml	salt	2 tbsp
30 ml	sunflower oil	2 tbsp
	2 red or green chillies, deseeded and thinly sliced	
1 cm	fresh ginger, peeled, sliced and shredded	½ in
25 g	soft light brown sugar	1 oz
45 ml	rice or herb vinegar	3 tbsp
5 ml	cornflour (cornstarch) mixed to a paste with water	1 tsp
15 ml	sesame oil	1 tbsp
	GARNISH:	
	A few toasted sesame seeds	

1. Peel the cucumbers with a potato peeler and cut in half lengthwise. Scoop out the seeds using a teaspoon. Slice into 1 cm/½ in pieces and sprinkle with salt. Set aside for 30 minutes then rinse with cold water and dry on kitchen paper.

2. Heat the oil in a warmed wok and fry the chillies and ginger for 30 seconds without browning. Add the cucumber pieces and stir-fry for 2 minutes.

3. Add the sugar and vinegar. Make the cornflour paste up to 300 ml/½ pt/1¼ cups with water and stir into the pan. Lower the heat, add the sesame oil and stir for 30 seconds.

4. Lift the cucumber into a serving dish and boil the sauce in the wok to reduce to a thin syrup. Pour it over the cucumber.

5. Cool and cover, then chill until required. Scatter with sesame seeds just before serving.

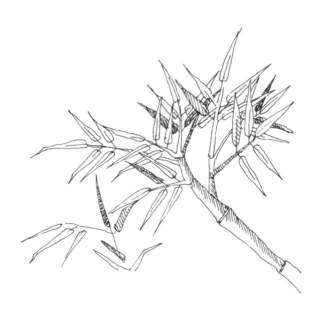

RICE AND NOODLES

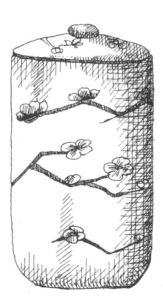

BOILED AND STEAMED RICE

You will find the instructions for cooking these on page 38.

EGG FRIED RICE

DAN CHAO FAN

In the Chinese kitchen, leftovers are transformed in no time into yet another delicious meal. Make sure that the rice is quite cold so that the grains remain separate when fried. As a guide 175 g/6 oz of uncooked rice will give the required 450 g/1 lb after cooking.

Serves 4

	1 small onion, finely chopped	
45 ml	groundnut (peanut) or sunflower oil	3 tbsp
	1 egg, beaten	
	Salt and freshly ground black pepper	
450 g	leftover cooked rice (see above)	1 lb
	3 spring onions (scallions), finely shredded	

1. Fry the onion in the wok in hot oil until just turning pale brown.

2. Add the beaten egg to the onion, stir to scramble the mixture. Season to taste. Break up and add the rice. Cook over a high heat, stirring all the time until the rice is hot and flecked with tiny pieces of the egg.

3. Turn on to a warm platter garnished with shredded spring onion. Serve at once with a variety of dishes.

SPECIAL FRIED RICE

SHI JIN CHAO FAN

*T*his could almost stand on its own as a brunch or supper dish
or alongside other dishes when you have a number of guests
and several items on the menu.

Serves 4

450 g	cold cooked rice	1 lb
	4 Chinese dried mushrooms, soaked in water for 30 minutes	
100 g	Chinese sausage, sliced (optional)	4 oz
90 ml	sunflower oil	6 tbsp
	1 egg, beaten	
	2 small onions, sliced	
	3 garlic cloves, crushed	
100 g	peeled prawns (shrimp), thawed if frozen	4 oz
100 g	cold roast pork or chicken, shredded (optional)	4 oz
15–30 ml	light soy sauce	1–2 tbsp
	Freshly ground black pepper	
100 g	frozen peas, thawed	4 oz
	2 spring onions (scallions), shredded	
	1 red chilli, deseeded and thinly sliced (optional)	
	A few fresh coriander (cilantro) leaves	

TO SERVE:

A little shredded lettuce

1. Fork the rice through and set aside.

2. Drain the mushrooms, discard the stems and slice the
caps thinly.

3. If using the Chinese sausage, place in a colander over hot water covered with a lid and steam for 10 minutes. Slice into thin rings.

4. Assemble all the other ingredients.

5. Heat 15 ml/1 tbsp of the oil in a small frying pan (skillet) and make a thin omelette with the beaten egg. Roll up like a sausage and cool before cutting into fine strips. Reserve.

6. Stir-fry the onions in a warm wok in some of the oil until just taking on a golden colour. Lift out and reserve.

7. Quickly stir-fry the garlic and prawns and also set aside.

8. Now fry the shredded pork or chicken, if using, and mushrooms.

9. Heat the remaining oil and when hot toss in the rice, stirring all the time. Add the soy sauce, seasoning and half of the reserved cooked ingredients.

10. Toss well, then add the peas and half the spring onion.

11. Serve on a warmed platter. Top with the rest of the cooked ingredients, the rest of the spring onion, the chilli and coriander leaves.

12. Surround the rice with a fringe of shredded lettuce and serve immediately.

SHREDDED CHICKEN FRIED RICE WITH CRISPY LETTUCE

JI SI CHAO FAN

superior fried rice which I first sampled at the Oriental Restaurant at the Dorchester. Serve alongside other dishes or on its own as a lunch or supper offering.

Serves 6

350 g	fragrant Thai rice, cooked and allowed to become cold	12 oz
150 g	chicken breast, skinned	5 oz
	Pinch of salt	
2.5 ml	sugar	½ tsp
5 ml	rice wine or dry sherry	1 tsp
5 ml	cornflour (cornstarch) mixed with 5 ml/1 tsp water	1 tsp
45 ml	oil	3 tbsp
	2 eggs beaten with 30 ml/2 tbsp water	
	¼ iceberg lettuce, shredded	
	4 spring onions (scallions), finely shredded	
	Salt and freshly ground black pepper	

1. Fork through the rice. Slice the chicken breast and cut into fine shreds. Place in a bowl with the salt, sugar, rice wine or sherry and cornflour paste.

2. Heat the wok, add half the oil and when hot fry the chicken shreds until they change colour and are tender. Lift out and keep warm.

3. Heat the remaining oil and add the eggs quickly followed by the rice and stir so that the egg is well distributed.

4. Add most of the lettuce and spring onions and season to taste. When very hot turn on to a serving platter and garnish with the remaining lettuce and spring onions.

MANDARIN NOODLES

LIANG BAN MEIN

Served as a light lunch or supper or as part of a buffet, this noodle dish with crisp cucumber and bean sprouts topped with a sesame flavoured dressing is a delightful blend of textures and flavours. Add a few drops of oil to the water for boiling the noodles to keep the strands separate.

Serves 6

	1 cucumber, halved lengthwise	
	Salt	
225 g	dried noodles or wholewheat spaghetti	8 oz
15 ml	sesame seeds, toasted	1 tbsp
100 g	bean sprouts	4 oz
	4 spring onions (scallions), white part chopped and tops cut into slivers	
100 g	cold roast pork, finely shredded (optional)	4 oz
	DRESSING:	
60 ml	groundnut (peanut) or sunflower oil	4 tbsp
15 ml	sesame oil	1 tbsp
30 ml	light soy sauce	2 tbsp
5 ml	sugar	1 tsp
	Freshly ground black pepper	

1. Scoop the seeds from the cucumber halves using a teaspoon. Cut into 4 cm/1½ in lengths and then into fine matchstick-like pieces. Sprinkle with salt and set aside for 15 minutes.

2. Cook the noodles for 5 minutes or until just tender, but with a little bite. Drain, refresh with cold water and set aside to drain thoroughly. Cook spaghetti according to packet instructions.

3. Dry-fry or toast the sesame seeds and reserve.

4. Blend the oils, soy sauce and sugar with black pepper to taste.

5. Toss the noodles with the cucumber, bean sprouts, white part of the spring onions and pieces of pork, if using. Pour over the prepared dressing when ready to serve.

6. Turn on to a serving platter and garnish with the spring onion slivers and toasted sesame seeds.

SZECHUAN NOODLES WITH PEANUT SAUCE AND VEGETABLES

DANG DANG MEIN

he noodles in this dish are served tossed with the sesame flavoured dressing but separately from the vegetables. Each person takes a helping of noodles, then adds a selection of the chopped vegetables. It's fun to serve and an ideal vegetarian dish. It is reminiscent of Thamin lethok, a Burmese noodle dish, which I enjoyed in Rangoon and which is served in exactly the same way. This neatly illustrates how foods migrate from one country to another and yet are considered a particular speciality of each nation.

Serves 4 as a lunch, or more as part of a meal

450 g	fresh egg noodles or fresh tagliatelle OR	1 lb
225 g	dried noodles	8 oz
	½ cucumber, sliced lengthwise, deseeded and diced	
	Salt	
	4-6 spring onions (scallions), thinly sliced	
	½ moolie, peeled and coarsely grated OR	
	1 bunch radishes, roots trimmed and sliced	

100 g	bean sprouts, rinsed then left in iced water	4 oz
60 ml	groundnut (peanut) or sunflower oil	4 tbsp
	2 garlic cloves, crushed	
45 ml	sesame paste (tahini) OR	3 tbsp
75 ml	crunchy peanut butter	5 tbsp
15 ml	sesame oil	1 tbsp
15 ml	soy sauce	·1 tbsp
5-10 ml	chilli sauce	1-2 tsp
15 ml	vinegar	1 tbsp
60-75 ml	chicken stock or water	4-5 tbsp
	Sugar to taste	

GARNISH:
A few peanuts, crushed

1. Cook fresh noodles in boiling water for 1 minute (or 4-5 minutes for fresh tagliatelle) then drain, rinse and drain well. Cook dried noodles as suggested on page 181 or according to packet directions.

2. Sprinkle the cucumber with salt and set aside for 15 minutes to bring out the juices then rinse and dry on kitchen paper.

3. Prepare the spring onions, mooli or radishes and bean sprouts which should be drained well. Arrange either in a separate bowl or in piles on a serving dish.

4. Assemble all the other ingredients and when ready to eat, heat 30 ml/2 tbsp of the oil and fry the noodles quickly, stirring constantly for 1 minute. Lift into a serving bowl with a draining spoon and keep warm.

5. Add the remaining oil to the wok and fry the garlic to flavour the oil. Remove from the heat and stir in the sesame paste or peanut butter with the sesame oil, soy and chilli sauces, vinegar, stock or water and a little sugar to taste. Stir well together and just warm through over a gentle heat.

6. Pour over the noodles in the bowl and toss well. Garnish with crushed peanuts and serve with the prepared vegetables.

EGG NOODLES WITH ROAST PORK

CHAR SUI TANG MEIN

Noodles are China's fast food and are served in soups, stir-fry or deep-fried dishes. The dried egg noodles are reconstituted for stir- or deep-frying by plunging into boiling water and cooking for about 5 minutes. Drain, rinse and drain again, then use as directed. You can also place the noodles into boiling water, return to the boil and then remove from the heat and allow to stand for 6 minutes. Always read the instructions on the pack before cooking.

Serves 4, or more as part of a meal

225 g	egg noodles, either fresh or dried and prepared (see above)	8 oz
100 g	roast pork or duck meat, cut into strips	4 oz
100 g	Chinese cabbage or leaves, shredded	4 oz
100 g	bean sprouts	4 oz
45 ml	oyster sauce	3 tbsp
15 ml	light soy sauce	1 tbsp
5 ml	sugar	1 tsp
	Salt and freshly ground black pepper	
60 ml	groundnut (peanut) or sunflower oil	4 tbsp
	2 garlic cloves, crushed	
120 ml	stock or water	4 fl oz/½ cup
	6 spring onions (scallions), shredded	
	1 red chilli, deseeded and thinly sliced	

1. Prepare the noodles and set aside with the meat.

2. Prepare the cabbage and bean sprouts. Blend the oyster and soy sauces together with the sugar and seasoning.

3. When all the ingredients are assembled, warm the wok, add the oil and when hot fry the garlic to flavour the oil but do not allow to brown.

4. Increase the heat, toss in the cabbage and bean sprouts, stir well then add the meat and stir constantly for 1 minute.

5. Add the stock or water then the noodles and cook for 1 minute.

6. Stir in the sauce mixture and most of the spring onions then cook over a high heat for 30 seconds. Turn on to a serving dish and garnish with remaining spring onions and chilli. Serve immediately.

FRIED NOODLES WITH SHREDDED ROAST DUCK

SHAO YA CHOW MEIN

C̸how Mein probably stirs memories of the very first Chinese restaurant you ever visited and is one of the Chinese cuisine's most adaptable dishes. It's a magic way of making a little go a long way; use whole prawns, tiny strips of fresh beef or pork fillet or chicken or indeed little strips of cooked meat from the weekend roast. The noodles are first par-boiled and are then subsequently fried in the juices from quickly cooking the other ingredients, half of which are stirred into the noodles and the remainder used as a garnish.

Serves 4–6

450 g	wheat flour noodles (or spaghetti)	1 lb
	6 Chinese dried mushrooms, soaked in water for 30 minutes	
175 g	roast duck meat, shredded	6 oz
	2 leeks, thinly sliced	
	2 sticks celery, thinly sliced	
1 cm	ginger, peeled and finely shredded	½ in
60 ml	groundnut (peanut) or sunflower oil	4 tbsp
45 ml	light soy sauce	3 tbsp
30 ml	rice wine or sherry	2 tbsp
	A little dark brown sugar	
	Salt and freshly ground black pepper	
	3 spring onions (scallions), chopped	

1. Par-boil the noodles for about 3 minutes, then drain well and set aside. (Cook spaghetti according to packet instructions.)

2. Drain the mushrooms, discard the stems and thinly slice the caps. Reserve the soaking liquid.

3. Prepare the duck pieces, leeks, celery and ginger. Assemble all the other ingredients.

4. Warm the wok, add the oil and when hot quickly fry the ginger to flavour the oil then add the leeks and celery and finally the duck meat, stirring constantly for 2 minutes. Lift out on to a plate.

5. Now fry the noodles in the remaining juices in the pan until they are very hot. Add the soy sauce, rice wine or sherry, sugar and seasoning.

6. Add half of the fried vegetable mixture with half of the spring onions and toss well then turn on to a serving platter.

7. Quickly heat the remaining vegetables and duck mixture and use to garnish the noodles. Scatter the remaining spring onions on top.

DESSERTS

PEKING DUST

LI TZE FENG

omething of a hangover from the days of the old colonials who lived in Peking in the 1920s, you can use fresh chestnuts if available and you have the time, or use a 350 g/12 oz can of whole, peeled, vacuum-packed chestnuts. Do not use the purée as the texture will be too mealy and bland.

Serves 4

450 g	whole chestnuts OR	1 lb
350 g	can whole peeled chestnuts	12 oz
	A little salt	
30-45 ml	sugar	2-3 tbsp
2.5 ml	vanilla essence (extract)	½ tsp
300 ml	whipping (heavy) cream ½ pt/1¼ cups	
A few pieces of preserved ginger, preserved pineapple and candied orange cut into neat slices		

1. If using fresh chestnuts, score on the base and place in a pan of boiling water and simmer for 40 minutes until cooked through. Drain, cool slightly, then peel.

2. Chop chestnuts reasonably finely by hand or with great care in a food processor so that the mixture still has some texture.

3. Mix the chestnuts with salt and sugar and make either one mound in a serving bowl or individual moulds in serving dishes.

4. Add the vanilla essence to the cream and whip until it holds its shape. Cover the chestnut mixture with cream.

5. Decorate with preserved fruits and chill.

GLAZED TOFFEE APPLES AND

BA TSU PING GUO

GLAZED TOFFEE BANANAS

BA TSU XIANG JIAO

esserts are not a great feature of a Chinese meal, as you will have noticed when perusing the menu. Sweet foods are more often served as a snack between meals. However, the clever Chinese recognise that we Westerners think a meal incomplete without a sweet ending and where they might only serve some fresh fruit they indulge us in a dish of toffee apples which are truly scrumptious. Bananas, peeled and cut into halves or thirds, can be prepared in the same way. Allow 1 small banana per person. As this requires quite a lot of last minute attention, I would suggest that you have a trial run, perhaps cooking for four maximum, then you will be more confident to cook for more in due course.

Serves 6–8

	FRITTER BATTER:	
100 g	plain (all-purpose) flour 4 oz/1 cup	
15 ml	cornflour (cornstarch)	1 tbsp
1.5 ml	salt	¼ tsp
120–150 ml	water 4–5 fl oz/½–⅔ cup	
30 ml	groundnut (peanut) oil	2 tbsp
	2 egg whites	

	4 crisp eating apples	
15 ml	plain (all-purpose) flour	1 tbsp
	Oil for deep-frying	
225 g	granulated sugar	8 oz
60 ml	water	4 tbsp
	A few toasted sesame seeds	
	Iced water	

1. Prepare the batter by sifting the flour, cornflour and salt together. Slowly stir in the water and oil to make a smooth batter. Set aside with the egg whites at room temperature until required.

2. Prepare all the other ingredients but peel, core and cut the apples into eighths only when ready to start cooking, otherwise they will turn brown. Dust the apple or banana pieces with the flour.

3. Heat the oil to 190°C/375°F. Whisk the egg whites and fold into the batter. Pierce each apple or banana piece on a skewer and dip into the batter then fry in hot oil until golden brown. Fry in batches and drain on kitchen paper.

4. Heat the sugar and water in a heavy pan, stirring all the time until the sugar dissolves. When the caramel becomes pale golden, remove from the heat.

5. Dip the fritters in the caramel and transfer to oiled bowls to prevent sticking. Sprinkle with sesame seeds.

6. Place a large bowl of iced water on the table so that guests can dip the fritters in this to harden the caramel.

FRUIT MOUNTAIN

SHI JIN SHUI GUO PAN

really stunning display of fruit arranged on a 'mountain' of ice cubes will delight your guests. The pieces of fruit are cut much larger than we would serve in a fruit salad. Give everyone a cocktail stick so that they can help themselves from the 'mountain'. The quantity below is just generous for 4 people and will serve as a guide. Use whatever fruit is in season as the Chinese do, bearing in mind colour, texture and flavours.

Serves 4

	1 apple, peeled if liked, cored and cut into eight	
	Lemon juice	
	2 large oranges, peeled and segmented	
	1 small melon, chanterais or galia, cut in half, seeds removed	
	8 lychees, peeled or use canned when out of season	
225 g	black seedless grapes	8 oz
225 g	large strawberries	8 oz
	Plenty of ice cubes, slightly crushed	
	Sugar	

1. Prepare the fruits, leaving the pieces quite large. Toss apples in lemon juice to prevent discolouration. Either use a melon baller on the flesh of the melon or remove peel and cut into wedges. Do not remove hulls from strawberries.

2. Arrange ice cubes on a glass or silver platter or bowl for best effect and top with the pieces of fruit.

3. Hand round a bowl of sugar for guests with a sweet tooth.

ACKNOWLEDGEMENTS

RESTAURANTS

Joy King Lau
3 Leicester Street, London WC2H 7BL. Tel: 0171-437 1132/3

Kaifeng
51 Church Road, London NW4 4DU. Tel: 0181-203 7888

The Oriental Restaurant
The Dorchester, Park Lane, London W1A 2HJ. Tel: 0171-629 8888

The Panda Sichuen Restaurant
56 Old Compton Street, London W1V 5PA. Tel: 0171-437 2069

ORIENTAL STORES AND SUPERMARKETS

Any of the ingredients required for the recipes in this book will be found easily in China Town in London's Soho or wherever there is a Chinese community, no matter how small. Over the past few years Wing Yip has opened a series of stores which will provide you with all your culinary needs.

W. Wing Yip (London) Ltd, 395 Edgware Road, Cricklewood, London NW2 6LN. Tel: 0181-450 0422

375 Nechells Park Road, Nechells, Birmingham B7 5NT. Tel: 0121-327 6618

Oldham Road, Ancoats, Manchester M4 5HU. Tel: 0161-832 3215

550 Purley Way, Croydon CR0 4RF. Tel. 0181-688 4880

Wang Thai Supermarket is my local friendly store which sells a wide range of ingredients, fresh, dried and frozen. Fresh supplies of spices and vegetables are flow in from Thailand on a weekly basis.
101 Kew Road (near the Richmond roundabout), Richmond, Surrey TW9 2PN. Tel: 0181-332 2959

Talad Thai is another excellent local store run by Mr Kreignsak which sells a wide range of fresh, frozen and dried ingredients required for oriental cooking. 320 Upper Richmond Road, London SW15 6DL. Tel: 0181-788 8077

In addition, I have had generous help in samples from Tilda, having used Thai Jasmine rice in testing throughout. Cherry Valley Farms in Lincolnshire have provided duckling. They supply the majority of ducks to the Chinese stores in the UK.

Sharwoods are a highly regarded food company who sell a huge and ever-expanding range of oriental foods.

INDEX